OPERATION
DRAGON

INSIDE THE KREMLIN'S SECRET WAR ON AMERICA

AMBASSADOR R. JAMES WOOLSEY

LT. GEN. ION MIHAI PACEPA

Encounter
BOOKS

New York • London

First American edition published in 2021 by Encounter Books, an activity of Encounter for Culture and Education, Inc., a nonprofit, tax exempt corporation. Encounter Books website address: www.encounterbooks.com

Manufactured in the United States and printed on acid-free paper. The paper used in this publication meets the minimum requirements of ANSI/NISO Z39.48–1992 (R 1997) (*Permanence of Paper*).

FIRST AMERICAN EDITION

LIBRARY OF CONGRESS CATALOGING-IN-PUBLICATION DATA

Names: Woolsey, R. James, 1941– author. | Pacepa, Ion Mihai, 1928– author.
Title: Operation dragon : inside the Kremlin's secret war on America / by Ambassador R. James Woolsey and Lt. Gen. Ion Mihai Pacepa.
Description: New York : Encounter Books, [2021]
Includes bibliographical references and index.
Identifiers: LCCN 2020020632 (print) | LCCN 2020020633 (ebook)
ISBN 9781641771450 (cloth) | ISBN 9781641771467 (epub)
Subjects: LCSH: Espionage, Russian--United States--History.
Intelligence service—Soviet Union—History. | Spies—Soviet Union.
Classification: LCC JN6529.I6 W66 2021 (print) | LCC JN6529.I6 (ebook)
DDC 327.1247073—dc23
LC record available at https://lccn.loc.gov/2020020632
LC ebook record available at https://lccn.loc.gov/2020020633

Design of Developing the Secret Ink (photographic insert) by ADLI, LLC / Dana Bart

Interior page design and typesetting by Bruce Leckie

In Memory of Nancye Miller and Maurice Anthony Miller,
with love and admiration

To Mary Lou Pacepa,
who helped me to look at my past with American eyes

If you know the enemy and know yourself,
you need not fear the result of a hundred battles.
If you know yourself but not the enemy,
for every victory gained you will also suffer a defeat.
If you know neither the enemy nor yourself,
you will succumb in every battle.

—Sun Tzu, *The Art of War*

CONTENTS

INTRODUCTION

Until its wars against communist expansion in Korea and Vietnam, America was accustomed to victory. From 1776 to 1782 and in 1812, America gained and maintained its liberty from the British Empire, the most powerful in the world. In 1846, Mexico attacked and was soundly defeated. In 1898, the United States went to war to keep Cuba independent of Spain, decimating the Spanish fleet and forcing Spain to sue for peace. In World War I, in which over 40 million Europeans were killed, the United States quickly put together an army of 4 million and became instrumental in defeating the German aggressor. In World War II, almost half a million Americans died to defeat Nazism. At its end, a united America rebuilt her vanquished enemies. It took seven years and trillions of dollars to turn Hitler's Germany, Mussolini's Italy, and Hirohito's Japan into prosperous democracies, but the effort made the United States the uncontested leader of the world, a fact that has kept the peace for over seventy years.

America has always stood against tyranny from any ideological source. Russia during its socialist period killed over 90 million people throughout its empire. It stole American nuclear technology. It murdered one of our presidents. It generated today's international terrorism. Now, our intelligence professionals say, it openly interferes in America's internal affairs. This book is about why confronting such behavior must be at the center of America's foreign policy.

This is the first and it will be surely the last book in history to be co-written by a former director of the U.S. foreign intelligence community and an ex-Soviet–bloc spy chief. As communism collapsed economically in the early 1990s, Pacepa effectively sent a socialist tyrant, Nicolae Ceausescu of Romania, to the gallows by writing a book entitled *Red Horizons*. Knowledge is power. This book adds to our knowledge base about Russia as it was in the Soviet period and as it continues to be.

Karl Marx's *Communist Manifesto* has turned 172 years old, leaving behind the wreckage of nations like trailer parks after a hurricane. Communism's late socialist leaders are today reviled universally as tyrants, from the Soviet Union's Vladimir Lenin and Joseph Stalin to Cuba's Fidel Castro; from Yugoslavia's Josip Broz Tito to Bulgaria's Todor Zhivkov; from Albania's Enver Hoxha to Hungary's Mátyás Rakosi; from Guinea's Sékou Touré to Tanzania's Julius Nyerere and Venezuela's Hugo Chavez. For years the USSR's Nikita Khrushchev and Romania's Nicolae Ceausescu were even found unworthy of a marked grave.

The United States fought the Cold War for forty-four long years. It may have won, but unlike other wars, this war didn't end with the defeated enemy throwing down its weapons. The Soviet Union has changed its name, but at 6,612,100 square miles, Russia is still the largest country on earth geographically. It also still has the world's largest stockpile of nuclear and bacteriological weapons and the world's second largest fleet of ballistic nuclear missile submarines, a fact our politicians and press tend to ignore. Russia remains largely a mystery to America, but it is a puzzle that we assume away as subdued, or as having "collapsed," at our peril.

On March 16, 2014, Moscow state television announced with fanfare that Russia could now turn its archenemy, the U.S., into "radioactive ash." A single Russian electromagnetic pulse (EMP) nuclear bomb launched above the U.S. mainland from a fishing boat off either our East or West Coast could collapse the entire United States electric grid and all that depends on it—communications, transportation, banking, finance, and food and water. This is all that is currently necessary to sustain modern civilization and the lives of 360 million Americans. NATO's deputy supreme commander in Europe, General Sir Adrian Bradshaw, warned that "the threat from Russia and the risk it brings of miscalculation resulting in a strategic conflict represents an existential threat to our whole being." We agree.

The two of us have spent decades managing the foreign intelligence communities of our native countries. Behind Russia's new smiling face lurk almost a hundred nuclear and bacteriological cities built and managed by the KGB. This intelligence service has been rechristened the FSB only to make it seem to be a new organization. Its sole task is to steal U.S. military technologies and weapons and to secretly reproduce them as if they were Russian inventions. Chelyabinsk city in the Urals is on a map of the

Soviet Union. But Chelyabinsk-40, a city of 40,000 people also located in the Urals, is not. Nor do any maps show Chelyabinsk-65, Chelyabinsk-70, Chelyabinsk-95, or Chelyabinsk-115, all in the Urals. Krasnoyarsk city is in eastern Siberia, but there is no mention anywhere of Krasnoyarsk-25, Krasnoyarsk-26, or Krasnoyarsk-45. All these secret cities maintained by the KGB/FSB survived the collapse of the Soviet Union.[1]

Candidates for public office routinely ignore the threat to national security from historical enemies of the United States. Some appear to believe that Russia is now Westernized—some who lean left even seem to believe that Russia's cast-off socialism still ought to serve as a model for the United States. In the tradition of pie-in-the-sky promises, candidates for public office promise American voters Russian-style jobs, free education, and free health care for all. Few seem to grasp that the Soviet Union's economic disintegration in 1989 was final proof of socialism's bankruptcy as a system. Its failure also came without warning. Former CIA Director Stansfield Turner wrote in *Foreign Affairs* in 1991 that "I never heard a suggestion from the CIA or the intelligence arms of the departments of Defense or State" about "growing, systemic economic problems in the Soviet Union."[2] Rather, the trendy political science theory of the 1970s was "convergence." That the Soviet Union and the U.S. were more alike than different and were gradually coming together in a "convergence" of free market and socialist systems.

Our contemporary politicians do not seem to understand, or to remember, that each long war brings significant social and political changes to the belligerents. The Great War brought Marxism to Russia to create the Soviet Union. At the end of World War II, the USSR created a Marxist empire by swallowing up Eastern Europe. Right in the middle of the twentieth century, when much of the world was finally beginning to enjoy economic prosperity, Eastern Europe was shoved back into dismal feudalism.

In 1945, young British voters, tired of five years of war, kicked the legendary Winston Churchill—instrumental in winning World War II—out of office and brought in Clement Attlee, an undercover Marxist leader of the Labour Party. Attlee started his reign with a populist move: he nationalized the health care system and the finance system. Attlee went on, *l'appétit vient en mangeant,*[3] to nationalize the auto and coal industries, communication facilities, civil aviation, electricity, and the steel industry. The British economy collapsed, and the powerful British Empire passed into history. This history should have been a stern warning to all. But it was largely ignored. Marxists continued to flourish and to nurture their favorite idea. Now, after eighteen years of war in Afghanistan, the specter of Marx haunts even the United States. Young Americans too love the promise of a "free lunch."

The cover of *Newsweek* magazine just after our 2008 financial crisis proclaimed, "We Are All Socialists Now."[4] An article in, of all places, Russia's *Pravda*, declared, "It must be said, that like the breaking of a great dam, the American descent into Socialism is happening with breathtaking speed, against the backdrop of a passive, hapless sheeple, excuse me dear reader, I meant people."[5] A couple of years later, *Newsweek* was sold for a dollar, 14 million Americans had lost their jobs, and 41.8 million people had gone on government food stamps.

Therefore, we two decided to write a brief analysis about the secret role played by Russian intelligence in the free world. Russia has now become the first intelligence dictatorship in history—and few people know what that really means.

This is not just another spy story. It is a book about some of Russia's most successful anti-American espionage and disinformation operations. Through these operations, the KGB, now rebaptized as the FSB to look like a new organization, moved into the Kremlin. As a result, the KGB/FSB now owns Russia. Most of these operations were born during Stalin's and Khrushchev's Cold War years and were left in place, largely unaffected by the collapse of the Soviet economy and the Soviet political superstructure.

The Cold War years of Khrushchev and Andropov were the period in which KGB general Aleksandr Sakharovsky, at that time known to General Pacepa under an alias (as was the rule in those days), served as Romania's chief KGB adviser. Sakharovsky was a Soviet version of the heads of Mossad and MI6 at the peak of the Cold War. At that time, not even the members of the Israeli and British governments knew the identities of the heads of their secret intelligence agencies. Now very few people know that the urbane fan of classical music, Sakharovsky, who was also secrecy incarnate, was a killer. It is even less understood that under Khrushchev, Sakharovsky spread the KGB's domestic mass killings out into the West. During his fourteen years as the Soviet Union's top spy chief, the blood-thirsty Sakharovsky worked with the equally bloodthirsty Khrushchev to export Soviet-style communism to Cuba (1958–1962), where again, tens of thousands were killed to establish communist rule. Khrushchev's and

Sakharovsky's Cuban Missile Crisis (1962) brought the world to the brink of nuclear war. In 1969 Sakharovsky transformed airplane hijacking into a primary tool of international terrorism. That terrorist weapon of choice would resurface once again in New York City on September 11, 2001.

In this book we also focus on Russia's secret theft of America's super-secret nuclear technologies just before the era of Sakharovsky and Khrushchev. This theft of data helped Russia create today's nuclear risks by proliferating nuclear technology to communist China, North Korea, Pakistan, and probably beyond.

For the past eighteen years, Russia has been managed by undercover KGB officers. As a result, even its official policies, like most intelligence operations, have been effectively written in secret ink. Without the secret developing solution, such operations cannot be read. Combining our collective experience as a former head of foreign intelligence in the United States and a former acting chief of foreign intelligence of a Soviet bloc country, Romania, we have been in a position to decode a number of top-secret Soviet intelligence operations conducted against the United States that reveal the unseen face of today's Russia openly managed by its rechristened KGB, the FSB.

CHAPTER 1

SOCIALIST RUSSIA: AN "ILLEGAL" INTELLIGENCE TYRANNY

On September 20, 2004, a senior Democratic Party figure running for the White House said during a PBS radio interview with Jim Lehrer: "Well, let me just say quickly that I've had an extraordinary experience of watching up close and personal that transition in Russia, because I was there right after the transformation. And I was probably one of the first senators…to go down into the KGB underneath Treblinka Square and see reams of files with names on them. It sort of brought home the transition to democracy that Russia was trying to make."

We understand that confusing Treblinka, a Nazi death camp in Poland, with the KGB headquarters at the Lubyanka, in Moscow, could have been a slip of the tongue. But the fact that a main runner for the White House thought that he could claim to understand Russia because he had, on a junket, viewed a few KGB archive files written in a language he could not read, is scary. To romanticize the Russian danger leaves us unprepared to face its reality.

In 2010, the FBI arrested ten Russian illegal intelligence officers, otherwise known as spies, in the U.S. But President Barack Obama and Secretary of State John Kerry deported them to Russia before they were thoroughly interrogated by the FBI about their activities.[1]

The American media tends to treat the idea of illegal officers akin to a joke—comic book characters, spy novel fodder, or inconsequential sleepers. For the intelligence community, however, illegals are a particu-

7

larly insidious and dangerous component of espionage. To preserve the secrecy of these agents, the Kremlin goes to dramatic lengths. One example was the dramatic prison break in England on October 22, 1966, of George Blake, a former ranking officer of the British foreign intelligence service (SIS). He had been considered by his superiors as a possible "C" (chief of the entire British foreign intelligence). Sprung from Wormwood Scrubs prison, he was never seen again in the West. Blake was serving an unprecedented forty-two-year sentence for having compromised the West's highly secret "Operation Gold" to the KGB—a tunnel in East Berlin used to tap Soviet military telephone lines during the Cold War—and the identities of some four hundred SIS and CIA officers and agents involved in that secret operation. After a tip from a Soviet bloc defector, Blake was arrested and sentenced for espionage. As far as we know, the British SIS did not then suspect that Blake was a Soviet illegal officer.

Forty-four years later, a former head of the KGB, Vladimir Putin, installed himself as Russia's president. Two years after that, a select cluster of former senior KGB officers gathered at Lubyanka, the headquarters of the KGB, to launch George Blake's book *Transparent Walls*. Sergey Lebedev, the new head of Russia's Foreign Intelligence Service (SVR), wrote in the book's foreword that, despite the book being devoted to the past, it was about the present. Blake's book was, indeed, a message to all Russian illegal officers around the world: it is again your time.

The term "illegal" has a specialized meaning. Intelligence officers working under the cover of official representatives, such as diplomats, in foreign countries are "legal," overt "spies." Officers documented as natives of a foreign target country and embedded in that country for the rest of their operational lives are "illegals."

Illegal officers might just be your next-door neighbors. They are documented as born in your country, and they speak your language with native fluency. Some might be even ranking members of your country's administration, like George Blake. All, however, are ready to become operationally active on special occasions, such as for killing political opponents, influencing elections, or replacing the legal agents in times of war when the enemy's embassies are shut down. Some are even prepared to create skeletons of pro-Russian governments in that country after the end of major wars.

In May 1974, the chancellor of West Germany, Willy Brandt, wrote to

the West German president: "I accept political responsibility for negli-
gence in connection with the Guillaume espionage affair and declare my
resignation from the office of federal chancellor."[2] Günter Guillaume was
an illegal officer of Communist East Germany's Stasi intelligence service[3]
who had risen to become a staunch member of the West German SPD
party and a trusted adviser to Brandt himself. Sentenced to thirteen years
in prison, in 1988 he was returned to East Germany in exchange for Western spies caught in the Eastern bloc. In East Germany, Guillaume was
celebrated as a hero. There he published his bestselling autobiography,
Die Aussage (The Statement).

KGB officer Panteleymon Bondarenko, aka "Pantyusha," the first chief
of Communist Romania's political police, the Securitate, starting in 1948,
told Pacepa (in vulgar terms) that illegals had changed the face of Europe.
Herbert Wehner, the West German SPD party chairman in the Bunde-
stag and minister for "all-German affairs" (meaning relations with East
Germany), pretended to have spent World War II as a political refugee in
Sweden. In fact, as Pacepa learned from Pantyusha, Wehner had sheltered
in Moscow, along with Walter Ulbricht, Matyas Rakosi, Georgi Dimitroff,
Klement Gottwald, and Boleslaw Bierut. All became illegal Soviet officers
charged to take over the governments of Eastern and Central Europe as
soon as those countries were "liberated" by the Red Army. All carried the
undercover rank of colonel except for Dimitroff, who became an "illegal"
general. "All secretly worked for us," Pantyusha explained, as Stalin did
not give a "fucking kopek" for any foreign communist in Moscow "who
tried to weasel out of working with us."

It is very hard to identify an illegal officer living in the West under a
Western biography. General Pacepa approved many of them. All carried
original Western birth certificates, school diplomas, pictures of alleged
relatives, and even fake graves of relatives in the West. In some important cases, the KGB community also created ersatz living relatives in the
West—ideologically motivated people who received life-long secret an-
nuities from the Soviet bloc intelligence community.

One of these illegals was so carefully documented that he rose to ambassador of an enemy nation. His Russian name was Iosif Grigulevich. At
the end of World War II, Stalin was at the peak of his glory, but he hated
Pope Pius XII, who in 1949 had excommunicated Stalin and his Communist Party. In retaliation, Stalin ordered an illegal to be tasked to kill Pope

Pius XII. Grigulevich, documented as Teodoro B. Castro, the supposed illegitimate son of a recently deceased wealthy Costa Rican, was selected because on February 22, 1947, the nephew of Pius XII, Prince Giulio Pacelli (birth name, Eugenio Pacelli) had become the Costa Rican minister plenipotentiary to the Holy See.

In 1949, Grigulevich and his Mexican KGB-recruited wife settled in Rome. He was now known as Teodoro Castro, a rich Costa Rican coffee merchant. Castro bought his way into the Costa Rican diplomatic service and by 1952 had risen to the post of Costa Rican minister plenipotentiary to Italy. KGB archivist Vasili Mitrokhin, who defected to the British in 1993 (and whose information has been described by the FBI as "the most complete and extensive intelligence ever received from any source"), reported seeing Grigulevich's personnel file in KGB archives with a note saying that as Castro he had "successfully cultivated the Costa Rican nuncio [sic] to the Vatican, Prince Giulio Pacelli, a nephew of Pope Pius XII" and "had a total of fifteen audiences with the Pope."

On March 5, 1953, Stalin unexpectedly died, and the illegal operation to assassinate Pope Pius XII was cancelled. In 1954, Grigulevich honorably retired from the KGB. Settling down in Moscow under the name Lavretsky, he died in 1988.

A contemporary version of Grigulevich in the United States may be Bob Avakian. An American citizen, Avakian was said to be living in self-exile in Paris where he was rarely sighted. Avakian owned "revolution bookstores" in sixteen American cities, including Cambridge, Berkeley, New York, and Seattle, and he published a Soviet-style anti-American magazine called *Revolution*. Some years ago, Avakian formed a Soviet-style Revolutionary Communist Party (RCP), which was instrumental in sparking the 1992 Los Angeles riots and more recently in creating two Soviet-style radical organizations, Not in our Name and World Can't Wait.

We do not yet have a contemporary source like Pacepa to tell us if Avakian is another Grigulevich. But Avakian is now at work on replacing the U.S. Constitution with a *Constitution for the New Socialist Republic in North America*, an American version of Lenin's *The State and the Revolution*, which turned Russia into the Gulag Archipelago.

The draft of Avakian's constitution is a disturbing read. Behind its supposedly American façade, the document is breathtaking in its Soviet-style brutality: "In order to bring this new Socialist Republic into being, it would be necessary to thoroughly defeat, dismantle and abolish the capitalist-imperialist state of the USA; and this in turn would only become possible with the development of a profound and acute crisis in society." The RCP Constitution legalizes "special Tribunals" for dealing with the "war crimes and other crimes against humanity" committed by "former members and functionaries of the ruling class of the imperialist USA and its state and government apparatus." These enemies of the state will "be imprisoned or otherwise deprived of rights and liberties."[4]

It is an echo of Khrushchev: "Stealing from capitalism is moral, Comrades," Khrushchev used to preach. "Don't raise your eyebrows, Comrades. I intentionally used the word steal. Stealing from our enemy is moral, Comrades." During the years Pacepa was his national security adviser, Ceausescu of Romania would also sermonize that stealing from capitalists was a Marxist duty. "Capitalists are the mortal enemies of Marxism," Pacepa heard Fidel Castro inveigh in 1972, when he spent a vacation in Cuba as a guest of Fidel's brother, Raul. "Killing them is moral, comrades!"

Was Avakian's constitution written for the 2020 elections? Hard to say.

It will not be easy to break Russia's five-century-old tradition of *samoderzhavie*, or tsarism run by political police. This was Russia's historical form of government, and it appears to continue to be. Nevertheless, man would never have learned to walk on the moon had he not first studied where the moon lay in the universe and what it was made of. That is what this book seeks to do.

CHAPTER 2

UNDERCOVER FEUDALISM IN THE TWENTIETH CENTURY

Russia was the first hell on earth that legitimized theft and the elimination of despised groups of wealthy people as tools of national policy under the doctrine of socialism. The "kulak" or bourgeois class was eliminated and its property redistributed to the victors of the November 1917 socialist revolution. The imperial family's wealth and rich Russians' land were seized by the new Communist Party, and the Russian economy was nationalized. Property rights were eliminated, and most of Russia's major property owners were killed.

In 1931, socialism became the only religion allowed in Russia. Stalin's political police dynamited the Cathedral of Christ the Savior—the site of the premiere in 1882 of Tchaikovsky's famous *1812 Overture*, a symphony written to give thanks to God and the heroes of the war against Napoleon. Some fifty thousand other Russian churches were also demolished. Some six hundred bishops, forty thousand priests, and one hundred and twenty thousand monks and nuns were killed.[1]

In the mid-1930s, the Communist Party itself was coopted by Stalin, who stole all the country's top-level positions and pinned them onto his chest. By the middle of the twentieth century, Russia had reverted to a dismal autocratic feudalism, nicknamed socialism.

In August 1939, Soviet killing and stealing moved abroad. By signing the Nazi-Soviet Nonaggression Pact, along with its secret protocol, Stalin made off with Lithuania, Estonia, Latvia, Bessarabia, northern

Bukovina, and portions of Poland and Finland. During World War II, Stalin shifted focus to stealing Western technologies. Lacking private ownership and the vitality of competition, Soviet technological progress stalled. So Stalin sought to steal whatever the Soviets could not invent on their own. After World War II, Stalin also netted all of Eastern Europe and helped engineer Mao's victory in China. A few years later, the Kremlin managed to dispossess more than a third of the world's population of their properties.

It was nothing new for Russia. The astute French observer Astolphe Louis-Léonor, aka Marquis de Custine, concluded in 1839 that "everything is deception" in Russia. Like the Romans, Custine noted, the Russians "have taken their sciences and their arts from foreign lands. They have intelligence, but theirs is an imitative mind and, consequently, more ironic than fertile—it copies everything and creates nothing."[2] The Soviet Union's satellites were forced to Russianize and rewrite history accordingly. In communist Romania, the national radio headquarters was located on Alexander Popov Street because Soviet history held that the Russian Popov, not Guglielmo Marconi, had invented the radio. In reality, Popov was an insignificant Russian physicist, who on May 7, 1895, had presented a paper on a wireless lightning detector based on the work of Marconi. The Soviet Union and its satellite countries were all required to celebrate that day as Radio Day.

Lenin, the leader of the Bolshevik Revolution, was an educated lawyer who spent most of his mature life (1900–1917) in Western Europe, where political parties played a dominant role. He therefore quite naturally conceived of everything in terms of political parties. In his fundamental theoretical work, *What Is to Be Done?* (1902), Lenin developed his theory that the proletarian communist revolution should be led by a political party that would act as the "vanguard of the proletariat." In his vision, that "party of a new type," to which he devoted twenty years to construct, was to be the revolution's mentor, leader, and guide. The other main Western-educated Soviet theorist, Leon Trotsky, went a step further: "The abolition of secret diplomacy is the primary condition of an honorable, popular, really democratic foreign policy."[3] After the October Revolution, Trotsky became the commissar of foreign affairs and later of war.

In October 1917, when Lenin returned to Russia to head his communist revolution, he found a country very different from the Europe in which he had matured politically. Unlike Marx's England and Germany, whose economic problems had been caused by the industrial revolution, Russia was an agricultural backwater. Though nominally freed by Alexander II in 1861, Russia's peasants had never really owned property or been allowed to make decisions for themselves. Feudal Russia had no relevant history of political parties, unlike England and Germany. Furthermore, the Russia at the center of Lenin's revolution had a long history as a political police state, back to the sixteenth century's Ivan the Terrible, a feudal lord who ruled through a personal political police or praetorian guard. Every Russian tsar built his own political police force, which, more than any other instrument of government, was used to keep the country quiet and under his or her control.

When Peter the Great ascended to the throne at the end of the seventeenth century, he set up a secret police loyal solely to himself, the Preobrazhensky Prikaz. So secret was this organization that the exact date of its creation is still a mystery. Following Ivan the Terrible's principle that "anyone who is not with me is a traitor," Peter unleashed his new instrument of power against whoever spoke out against him, from his own wife and the nobles who dared to defy him to drunks who made jokes at his expense. Peter even entrusted the Preobrazhensky Prikaz with luring his own son and heir, the tsarevich Aleksey, back to Russia from abroad and torturing him to death.

Months after Tsar Nicholas I took the throne, he established the Third Section of his Imperial Chancellery as his secret police. His 1845 Criminal Code laid down draconian penalties for anyone guilty of writing or spreading written or printed works or representations intended to arouse disrespect for sovereign authority or for the personal qualities of the sovereign. The law in Russia was therefore, quite expressly, that there was no freedom of speech in Russia and, moreover, that harboring any intention of speaking in any manner that the tsar did not like was criminal. It amounted to the institutionalization of political crime in Russia.

The more moderate Aleksandr II abolished his predecessor's Third Section but created his own Department of State Police. This body failed to save his life, however, for in 1881 he was assassinated with a primitive hand grenade. Yet Ivan the Terrible's political police persisted, in one form or another, throughout the history of Russia. At the time of the October

Revolution, it was called the Okhrana, founded in 1881 by Alexander II. Responsible only to the tsar, it had the power to search, imprison, and exile on its own sole authority entirely independently of Russian law.

It was natural for Lenin to integrate his plans into this centuries-old tradition. On December 20, 1917, only two months after his final return to Russia, Lenin created his own political police, the famous Cheka (*Vserossiyskaya Chrezvychaynaya Komissiya po Borbe s Kontrrevolyutsiyey i Sabotazhem, or All-Russian Extraordinary Commission for Combating Counterrevolution and Sabotage*), which became the parent organization for subsequent generations of political police organizations.

The Cheka's coat of arms consisted of a shield, for protecting the revolution against traitors, and a sword, for putting its edge to those traitors' necks. Thus, the roots of this emblem led back to the days of Ivan the Terrible rather than to the political ideology of Karl Marx. In 1917, Lenin described the Cheka as a temporary organization needed to subdue his domestic enemies and consolidate the rule of his party. It is nevertheless clear that he envisioned a key role for this organization from the beginning. The Russian word "cheka" means linchpin, and the Chrezvychaynaya Komissiya was surely so named to have its initials, pronounced Che Ka, convey that sense.

The Cheka was the most rapidly expanding Soviet organization. It had started out with twenty-three men, but within a couple of years it numbered over two hundred thousand. A 1993 book written by British writer John Costello and Russian intelligence officer Oleg Tsarev, based on original KGB documents, reports that in 1920 "the Cheka's total strength was approaching a quarter of a million, and that it outnumbered the peak strength of the Tsar's Okhrana by more than two to one." In 1921, Soviet Russia counted more Cheka officers than party members.[4]

Twenty-one million people were killed by Lenin's new political police during the first fifteen years of socialism in Russia, such that it is no wonder that the socialist Cheka's magazine was named *Krasnye Terror (Red Terror)*. Even more than the Spanish Inquisition, the socialist political police, under each of its numerous names, has been synonymous with killing. The Spanish Inquisition used to kill individuals they deemed to be heretics. The Soviet political police indiscriminately killed its faithful, its unfaithful, and its priests as well. But all in all, socialism—and only in Russia—killed three times more people than Nazism. The murder rate extended to China and other countries where the socialist experiment has been tried expands many times beyond that.

In an August 11, 1918, handwritten order demanding that at least one hundred kulaks (prosperous peasants) be hanged in the town of Penza to set an example, Lenin wrote with his own hand: "Hang (hang without fail, so the people see) no fewer than one hundred known kulaks, rich men, bloodsuckers... Do it in such a way that people for hundreds of [kilometers] around will see, tremble, know and scream out: they are choking and strangling to death these bloodsucking kulaks."[5]

A 1918 article published in *Red Terror* magazine under the signature of Martyn Ivanovich Latsis, a deputy of Felix Dzerzhinsky, the first head of the Cheka, explained: "We are not waging war against individuals. We are exterminating the bourgeoisie as a class." Latsis's instructions to the Cheka were equally conclusive. "During investigation," he wrote, "do not look for evidence that the accused acted in word or deed against Soviet power. The first questions that you ought to put are: To what class does he belong? What is his origin? What is his education and profession? And it is these questions that ought to determine the fate of the accused. In this lies the significance of the Red Terror."[6]

At Lenin's direction, the Soviet Union's first commissar of Public Health in 1918, Nikolai Semashko, organized the Soviet Union's "free" socialist health care system. Later it would play a major role in bankrupting the nation, as after the political police, it was the largest Soviet bureaucracy. The government takeover of health care killed even more people throughout the Soviet bloc than the Cheka did, and the effects are long-lasting. In today's Russia it is still normal to have two patients share the same hospital bed.

Lacking the vitality of private enterprise, medical progress stagnated. The Nobel Prize for Medicine tells the story in a nutshell. During the last century, the United States's free-market medical care system was awarded seventy-two Nobel prizes. The Soviet Union's socialized medical system got none. (Tsarist Russia did get one Nobel Prize for Medicine in 1904 for Ivan Pavlov's conditional reflex theory.)

Bribery was the second major nightmare the Semashko "free" health care system generated. Everyone in the Soviet system knew one had to "stimulate" the bureaucracy to get any medical care. If you needed surgery, you knew that the first thing you had to do was find out what size of bribe would be acceptable to the bureaucrats who could approve that particular surgery. In 2008, *The Lancet* medical journal reported that in Russia, each doctor and nurse still had "his or her little tax" and that "they all prefer cash in envelopes, of course." Nurses took 50 rubles ($2) to empty a bedpan and 200 rubles ($8) to give an enema. Surgical operations started at 300 rubles, but "the sky's the limit."

People in the United States are not used to *baksheesh*, but in the future, if our health care system is being run by bureaucrats, we will soon get the hang of it. It may not start out as blatant bribes, but soon bribery is sure to become the rule in one way or another. In France, for instance, the government bureaucracy recently introduced a €1 franchise on every medical consultation, described as a "contribution au remboursement de la dette sociale" (contribution to the repayment of the social debt). That was followed by an €18 franchise on "costly" medical procedures. Now French patients are learning that if they discreetly slip an envelope with cash into the pocket of the doctor's white lab coat hanging in his office, they will get more "attention." And a little extra attention may indeed be vital in a centralized system in which doctors are obliged by law to see sixty to seventy patients a day.

The 2007 Romanian movie *The Death of Mr. Lazarescu*, which won more than twenty international prizes, depicts the Semashko-style health care system through the heartbreaking true story of Constantin Nica, a retired Romanian engineer who had the misfortune of growing old in a country that still ran a nightmarish government health care system twenty years after its last Communist dictator was gunned down by his own people.

The fictional Mr. Lazarescu, gravely ill, is followed as a Romanian government ambulance shuttles him from one government-owned hospital to the next. At the first three hospitals, although the doctors determine that he does need urgent surgery, the bureaucracy refuses to take him in because he is too old and does not have enough money to bribe the hospital personnel. Mr. Lazarescu stubbornly refuses to give up, but at the fourth hospital, he dies after a delayed and botched surgery. (The real Mr. Nica was actually dumped onto a park bench and left there to die.) Mr. Lazarescu's real enemy was not his illness but the uncaring, authoritarian attitude so deeply ingrained in bureaucratic practice. The whole movie is so realistic that even *The New York Times*—a strong supporter of government-run health care—had to admit that the movie "absorbs you into its world."

The Death of Mr. Lazarescu might be required viewing for our contemporary candidates for public office as they ponder U.S. government health care for all. Romania's example may give them at least some food for thought.

Ronald Reagan once said that freedom is never more than one generation from extinction. Russia proved him right. Toward the end of his life, the ailing Lenin dictated a political "testament" dated December 25, 1922, in which he began by worrying that Stalin, "having become Secretary-General, has unlimited authority concentrated in his hands, and I am not sure whether he will always be capable of using that authority with sufficient caution."

In a postscript dated January 4, 1923, Lenin described Stalin as being "too crude" and called for him to be replaced as the leader of the Bolshevik Party by another communist who would be "more tolerant, more loyal, more polite and more considerate to the comrades, less capricious, etc."[7] A few months later, Lenin chose Leon Trotsky, at that time the war commissar, as the leader of the Bolshevik Party and his own successor. In self-defense, Stalin thereupon formed a coalition with Feliks Dzerzhinsky, the father of Russia's socialist secret police, which had successfully protected Lenin's dictatorship by arbitrarily executing a reported quarter of a million real and imagined enemies. Drawn up by Felix Dzerzhinsky himself, a *dezinformatsiya* ploy put the baton of succession firmly in Stalin's hands. In January 1924, when Lenin died, Trotsky happened to be away in the Crimea taking the cure. Dzerzhinsky made sure that he was misinformed about the date of the funeral. With his only rival far from Moscow, Stalin easily managed to place the crown on his own head. A few months later, he rewarded Dzerzhinsky's loyalty by making him a candidate member of the Politburo.

Over the years, Stalin made Dzerzhinsky an object of Communist veneration second only to Lenin, though he buried that cult deep in secrecy, as he did with all the really important things in the Soviet Union. Lenin was embalmed and put on display in Red Square. After Dzerzhinsky's death in 1926, a figure representing him—using death impressions of his face and hands and dressed in a Cheka uniform—was placed in a glass coffin and exhibited at the officers' club of what would later be called the

KGB, now the FSB.[8] Then, in December 1937, on the twentieth anniversary of the Cheka's founding, Stalin raised Dzerzhinsky to the rank of "knight of the revolution."

Stalin is long gone, but killings by political police are still alive. In all Eastern European countries "liberated" by Stalin's Red Army, the way to Soviet-style socialism was paved with killings. On February 2, 1945, for instance, the NKVD—which had openly taken over the whole Bulgarian military, police, and economy—executed three regents, twenty-two ministers, sixty-eight members of parliament, and eight advisors to King Boris after accusing them of being Nazi war criminals. In the following months, another 2,680 members of Bulgaria's "fascist" government were executed as war criminals, and 6,870 were imprisoned despite the fact that Bulgaria had never been at war with the Soviet Union and most of those leaders had been instrumental in eventually moving Bulgaria over to the Allies' side. These trials were so outrageous that in February 1950, Washington broke off diplomatic relations with Sofia.

In August 1998, Russian General Albert Makashov charged that American-paid Jewish Zionists were ruining the motherland. He called for the "extermination of all Jews in Russia," shouting in the Duma: "I will round up all the Yids [pejorative for Jews] and send them to the next world." Russian television replayed this clip over and over again, and on November 4, 1998, the Duma endorsed Makashov's pogrom. It voted (121 to 107) to defeat a parliamentary motion to censure his hateful statement. Eighty-three of the Communist Party's 132 members in the Duma voted for Makashov, and of the remainder all but one declined to vote. Just before this vote, a former Soviet spy chief, General Yevgeny Primakov, had become Russia's prime minister. At the November 7, 1998, demonstration marking the eighty-first anniversary of the October Revolution, crowds of former KGB officers showed their support for the anti-Semitic general, chanting "Hands off Makashov!" and waving signs with anti-Semitic slogans.[9]

When the KGB archives are finally opened in full, we will find that Soviet socialism was deeply anti-Semitic and killed many more Jews than Nazi Germany did. Totalitarianism always requires a tangible enemy. The Jews, who for centuries were not protected by the power of a nation-state, have always served as a convenient scapegoat for both Nazism and communism.

Nowadays, the general perception is that Nazi Germany was the cradle of anti-Semitism, and it is not easy to change that perception. Nevertheless, before the words "Nazi Holocaust" were on everyone's tongue, we had the Russian word "pogrom," which means massacre. To the ancient Greeks, a holocaust was simply a burnt sacrifice. Long before the 1930s, when the German Nazis invented the Jewish Holocaust, the Russian tsars conducted Jewish pogroms. Russia's first major pogrom against Jews took place on April 15, 1881, in the Ukrainian town of Yelisavetgrad, named for Empress Elizabeth. Russia's administration and army were experiencing grave disorders and gross corruption, and emissaries from St. Petersburg called for the people's wrath to be vented on the Jews. The impoverished peasants obliged.

The 1939 edition of an authoritative Russian dictionary defines pogrom: the government-organized mass slaughter of some element of the population as a group, such as the Jewish pogroms in tsarist Russia. Let us go back to the beginning. After 1492, when some of the Jews expelled from Spain by Queen Isabella began settling in Russia, they became involved in tax collection and the administration of large estates where peasants worked. Those were two of the few occupations Jews were allowed to pursue in tsarist Russia. Naturally, the new Jewish immigrants hardly made themselves loved in their new country.

In 1881, Tsar Alexander II was assassinated by a band of Nihilists. Alexander III, his successor, decided to save Russia from anarchy by transforming it into a nation containing only one nationality, one language, one religion, and one form of administration, and he began his new policy by instigating more Yelisavetgrad-style pogroms. A wave of killings, rapes, and the pillaging of Jews spread quickly to hundreds of other towns, reached Warsaw, and moved on to the rest of the Russian empire. The tsarist authorities held the victims responsible for the violence.

In an 1881 memorandum to Tsar Alexander III, the minister of interior, Count Nikolay Ignatyev, blamed the pogroms on "the Jews' injurious activities" directed against the peasantry. A tsarist investigative commission concluded: "The passion for acquisition and money-grabbing is inherent in the Jew from the day of his birth; it is characteristic of the Semitic race, manifest from almost the first page of the Bible."[10]

These anti-Semitic ideas were soon embodied in a document entitled *The Protocols of the Elders of Zion*, forged by Tsar Alexander III's newly created political police, the Okhrana.[11] To disguise its hand, the Okhrana claimed it to be the minutes of the first Zionist Congress (held in Basel, Switzerland in 1897), at which the Jews had allegedly plotted to take over the world.

The legendary head of the KGB *dezinformatsiya* department, General Ivan Agayants, introduced General Pacepa to the secrets of this unique forgery. The *Protocols* was originally compiled by the Okhrana to smear Russia's Jews who wanted to modernize the country and to limit the influence of its old aristocracy. The author of the *Protocols* was an Okhrana disinformation expert, Petr Ivanovich Rachovsky. Then assigned to France, he saw that the Dreyfus affair had divided France into two irreconcilable factions and aroused an enormous wave of anti-Semitism.[12] Rachovsky lifted most of his text from an obscure 1864 French satire called *Dialogue aux Enfers entre Machiavel et Montesquieu* (*Dialogue in Hell Between Machiavelli and Montesquieu*) by Maurice Joly, which accused Emperor Napoleon III of plotting to seize all the powers in French society. Rachovsky then merely substituted the words "the world" for France and "the Jews" for Napoleon III.

On October 20, 1894, Alexander III unexpectedly died of nephritis. This caused the Okhrana to sit on the *Protocols* until 1903, at which time it published them to bolster the weak tsar Nicholas II's hand against Jewish liberals who favored modernization in Russia. After the Russian Revolution of 1905, a constitution was promulgated and a Duma created. Count Sergey Witte, a former Okhrana target, became prime minister. The Okhrana then used the *Protocols* to undermine him, publishing it in Paris under the name of a mystic Russian priest, Sergius Nilus, as part of an anti-revolutionary propaganda campaign.

General Sakharovsky showed Pacepa a copy of the Nilus edition from the tsar's library. According to him, the *Protocols* had been the most resilient piece of disinformation in history. In 1921, the *Times* of London published a devastating exposure of the forgery by printing extracts from the *Protocols* side-by-side with plagiarized passages from the Joly book.[13] But that didn't stop the *Protocols* from becoming the basis for much of Hitler's anti-Semitic philosophy, as expressed in *Mein Kampf*, written in 1923. In fact, Nazi Germany translated the *Protocols* into many languages and flooded the world with it in support of its allegation that there was a

Jewish conspiracy aimed at world domination and that the persecution of Jews was a necessary tool of self-defense for Germany.

Now the *Protocols* has attained new prominence in the Arab and Islamic world.

CHAPTER 3

SOCIALIST ANTI-SEMITISM

talin, who succeeded Lenin to the Kremlin in 1922, hailed from the
remote land of Georgia. The Jews had traditionally been serfs in
Georgia until 1871, when serfdom was abolished there. Stalin's own
conventional Georgian anti-Semitism was simply transferred into national
policy carried out by his political police. When Stalin decided to eliminate
his main rival, Leon Trotsky (née Lev Davidovich Bronstein), his political
police were told to put together a *dezinformatsiya* operation portraying
Trotsky as a Jewish spy paid by American Zionism. He then expelled
Trotsky from the country. That allegation also served as justification for
Stalin to have Trotsky barbarically assassinated with an ice pick in Mexico
City, without even causing most of Russia to blink.

Next, Stalin sentenced to death the first chairman of the Comintern, Grigory Zinoviev (née Ovsel Gershon Aronov Radomyslsky). He
too had been born into a bourgeois Jewish family. Zinoviev was falsely
accused of organizing a Terrorist Center for the Assassination of Soviet
Government and the CPSU [Communist Party of the Soviet Union]
and shot.

The man named by Lenin in his testament as the most capable of the
younger generation, Georgy Pyatakov, was framed as a spy in the pay of an
invented American Zionist conspiracy. He too was shot. Out of the seven
members of Lenin's Politburo at the time of the October Revolution, only
Stalin was still alive when the massacre stopped. Even the wife of Vyacheslav

Molotov, Stalin's strongest political supporter and his prime minister since 1930, was exiled to Siberia for the sole reason that she was a Jew.

To maintain his position as feared boss over the new party stars starting to shine in Eastern Europe after World War II, Stalin periodically framed a few of them as tools of imperial-Zionist espionage services. He started the process in 1949 by organizing widely publicized show trials against the communist leaders of Hungary, Laszlo Rajk and Gyorgy Palfy. Both were sentenced to death. Three years later, Stalin's political police organized another show trial in Prague, at which the head of the Communist Party, Rudolf Slansky, and ten other party leaders, most of them Jews, were framed as Zionist spies and hanged. Next he kidnapped Hungary's Prime Minister Imre Nagy from Budapest and had him hanged as a Jewish spy. Imre Nagy was followed by Lucretiu Patrascanu, one of the founders of Romania's communist party, who was shot in the back of his head. Stalin asserted that these countries were on the verge of falling into imperial-Zionist clutches, so supposedly to preserve their socialist future, he had most of the Jews in Eastern Europe expelled from their communist parties. All in all, 21 million people are believed to have been killed by the KGB and its Eastern European sisters during Stalin's anti-Semitic purge, many framed as Zionist spies.[1]

After this consolidation of power by show trial and murder, Stalin made the Cheka answerable only to himself, just as the Okhrana and its predecessors had been responsible only to the tsar. Stalin then changed the name of Cheka into the GPU (*Gosudarstvennoye Politicheskoye Upravleniye*, or State Political Directorate). This name change was revealingly descriptive.

A U.S. State Department report released in September 1999 asserts that "Jews continue to encounter societal discrimination" in Russia. The report mentions numerous "major acts of intimidation linked to anti-Semitic groups in Russia," such as a large bomb exploded at the Marina Roscha Synagogue in Moscow on May 13, 1998, 149 graves desecrated at a Jewish cemetery in Irkutsk in May 1998, the Jewish synagogue in Novosibirsk destroyed by vandals in March 1999, and two bombs exploded simultaneously near the Marina Roscha Synagogue and the Moscow Choral Synagogue during the same year.[2]

On August 3, 2001, ninety-eight U.S. senators expressed concern about the resurgence of anti-Semitism in the Russian Federation in a letter sent to President Putin.[3] In January 2005, in a letter to the country's prosecutor general, nineteen members of the Duma accused the Jews of being on the payroll of American Zionism and asked that all Jewish organizations in Russia be banned. The letter compared Judaism to Satanism and accused Jews of ritual murders.[4] "Anti-Semitism in Russia has reached tremendous proportions," a 2006 survey stated, according to Abraham Hirschorn, a member of the Israeli cabinet. The 2006 report mentions a recent stabbing rampage against Moscow's synagogue goers and a Russian petition to outlaw Judaism.[5]

In June 2001, Vladimir Putin and his KGB officers, who had just taken over the Kremlin, in answer to the Lithuanian government's request for compensation to cover some of the damage caused by the Soviet occupation, brazenly asserted with a straight face that Lithuania and the other Baltic republics had "voluntarily" joined the Soviet Union in the face of the Nazi threat and that the USSR had sent its troops into the Baltic region only after the leaders there had requested it. This bold lie represented another effort to protect one of the Kremlin's best kept secrets: how the infamous Hitler-Stalin Pact of 1939 epitomized the organic connection between communism and Nazism in partitioning much of Europe between the Soviet Union and Nazi Germany. Entirely constructed by Stalin's political police, it constituted one of the most anti-Semitic *dezinformatsiya* operations carried out by the Kremlin. In 1938, Stalin was afraid that the British and French governments, to avoid war with the powerful German military machine, would quietly encourage Hitler to move eastward against the Soviet Union. To Stalin's eyes, the passivity with which London and Paris reacted to Hitler's annexation of Austria in March 1938 supported his fears. However, publicly, in 1935, at the Comintern's Seventh Congress, Stalin had made the defeat of fascism the Soviet Union's primary goal, following through by organizing international "popular fronts" against fascism. So to turn Nazi Germany into a Soviet ally, Stalin used clandestine diplomacy.

He began the operation by appointing fellow Georgian Lavrentiy Beria as head of the NKVD and tasking him to lure Hitler's Germany into becoming a Soviet ally. Stalin and Beria began by getting rid of the chief of the INO (*Innostranny Otdel*, the NKVD's foreign department), Mikhail Shpigelglas, who was Jewish, by having him poisoned. Next, they replaced Shpigelglas with another trusted fellow Georgian, Vladimir Dekanozov, whom Stalin had made deputy commissar of foreign affairs (i.e., deputy foreign minister) at the same time.

Once that was done, Stalin and Beria began purging the rest of the Jews from the INO and from the Commissariat for Foreign Affairs. In a few months, the five-foot Dekanozov, who as vice premier of Georgia had become known as "the hangman of Baku," arrested most of the INO's Jewish officers and framed them as Zionist spies. All were shot. Stalin and Beria then had him do the same in the Commissariat for Foreign Affairs. There, the last man to go was the foreign minister himself, Maksim Litvinov, née Meir Walach.

Stalin and Dekanozov completed their Jewish purge in the summer of 1938. They then let Hitler learn that Moscow was ready to give him oil, grain, cotton, and certain scarce metals such as chromium and manganese in exchange for a bilateral nonaggression treaty with Berlin. All the offered products were vital to Hitler's expansion plans, and to Stalin's satisfaction, Hitler apparently took the bait. The secret negotiations between Germany and the Soviet Union started in July 1939 in Berlin. Only Molotov of the Soviet delegation was not an INO officer. The delegation's permanent head was Dekanozov, who, together with a large staff of INO officers under diplomatic cover, spent the next two months in Berlin. Negotiations concluded on August 23, 1939, in Moscow, where Molotov and the German foreign minister, Joachim von Ribbentrop, signed the German-Soviet Nonaggression Pact, the secret protocol that partitioned Poland between the two signatories and gave the Soviets a free hand over Estonia, Latvia, Finland, Bessarabia, and Northern Bukovina.

German archive documents state that Stalin was euphoric that day. He told Ribbentrop: "The Soviet government takes this new pact very seriously. I can guarantee, on my word of honor, that the Soviet Union will not betray its partner."[6] At the 1940 May Day parade in Moscow, Dekanozov appeared at Stalin's right atop Lenin's mausoleum,[7] the highest honor ever accorded by the Kremlin to a head of the Soviet espionage service. And no wonder. Lithuania, Estonia, Latvia, Bessarabia, northern Bukovina, and portions of Poland and Finland were now Soviet property. As soon as the August 1939 pact and its secret protocol were signed, Stalin tasked his spy services to Sovietize his new properties. The Latvian chapter of this operation was headed by Andrey Vyshinsky, who later Sovietized Romania and Bulgaria. Vyshinsky was an NKVD officer who had worked under cover of public prosecutor during Stalin's purges. In 1939 Stalin transferred Vyshinsky to the INO, gave him the undercover position of deputy commissar for foreign affairs, and charged him with managing the "peaceful" incorporation of Latvia into the Soviet Union.

The Red Army occupied Latvia on June 17, 1940. The next day Vyshinsky arrived in Riga as Stalin's special envoy. There he forced Karlis Ulmanis, the Latvian president, to appoint a "people's government." According to the INO plan, only two members of the new government were to be openly avowed communists: the minister of interior and the chief of the national police.

After Vyshinsky succeeded in installing his government, he delivered a speech from the balcony of the Soviet embassy in Riga, assuring the population that Moscow did not have the slightest intention of including Latvia in the Soviet Union. A couple of days later, however, with the help of an INO group he had brought with him to Riga, Vyshinsky ordered his newly appointed Latvian chief of police to arrest President Ulmanis and the main leaders of the Latvian opposition and deport them to the Soviet Union. Then he forced the new "people's government" to schedule parliamentary elections in two weeks and set up a Working People's Bloc controlled by INO undercover officers to run the elections with a single list of candidates.

Vyshinsky's elections took place from July 14–15, 1940, without secret ballot. Only the counting of the vote was secret; it was conducted by the Ministry of Interior, now headed by Vyshinsky's man. The results claimed that 97.8 percent of the votes were for Moscow's candidates. Soon after that, a few Latvian communists working for the Comintern in Moscow whom Vyshinsky had brought with him launched the slogan "Soviet Latvia." Speaking again from the balcony of the Soviet Embassy, Vyshinsky expressed his hope that the newly elected people's parliament would fulfill the wish of that slogan. That, of course, was exactly what happened. On July 21, 1940, the malleable parliament proclaimed Latvia a Soviet republic, and two weeks later Moscow's Supreme Soviet incorporated it into the Soviet Union. "I worked with Comrade Vyshinsky on that operation," Sakharovsky used to tell Pacepa, "and in 1943 I became his deputy for Sovietizing Romania."

By the time Stalin incorporated Latvia into the Soviet Union, Germany had already conquered most of Europe. Now Stalin again feared that Hitler would turn his armies against the Soviet Union. Therefore, in August 1940, he sent Dekanozov to Berlin once more. His new task was to tempt Hitler to move against the United Kingdom instead of toward the East by offering him a secret trade agreement under which the Soviet Union would be instrumental in breaking the economic embargo the Western powers had imposed on Germany.

On September 27, 1940, Hitler concluded the Tripartite Pact with Italy and Japan. A week later Dekanozov was in Berlin again, and during a walk in the woods he let German foreign minister Joachim von Ribbentrop understand that Stalin was ready to join the Axis. On November 12, 1940, Stalin sent a Soviet delegation to Berlin to discuss the details of his future cooperation with the Berlin-Rome-Tokyo axis. Again, except for Molotov, all his envoys were intelligence officers: Beria, the chief of the NKVD; his deputy, General Vsevolod Merkulov; and the pygmy Dekanozov.

Stalin believed that those talks were successful, and on November 20, just before their end, he appointed the INO chief as Soviet ambassador to Germany. Dekanozov presented his letters of accreditation to Hitler on December 19, 1940, without knowing that on the previous day the Führer had approved Operation Barbarossa for the invasion of the Soviet Union, ordering his troops to be ready by May 15, 1941. On June 21, 1941, Hitler's armies crossed the Soviet border, and for the first few weeks, the assailants met no organized resistance from the Red Army.

The Soviet intelligence operation leading to the Hitler-Stalin Pact is one of the most embarrassing moments in the Kremlin's history. For one thing it demonstrates the Kremlin's Nazi-style anti-Semitism. This may be why soon after World War II, Stalin purged the word "Nazism" from the Russian political vocabulary, replacing it with "Fascism."

Stalin's successor, Nikita Khrushchev, framed the three main players of this operation—Beria, Merkulov, and Dekanozov—as spies and had them shot. "Dead men don't have memories," Sakharovsky told Pacepa at that time.

SOCIALIST INDUSTRIAL ESPIONAGE

Pacepa spent twenty-two years (1956–1978) managing or supervising Romania's slice of the Soviet bloc's scientific and technological (S&T) intelligence effort. During that period, the bloc's intelligence community developed the purloining of foreign science and technology into a fine art practiced by a very large and well-trained machine.

Stalin's effort to Europeanize the Soviet Union was born in 1943 at the height of preparations for the Red Army's decisive offensive against Nazi Germany. Like everything else in socialist Russia, it was built on a foundation of theft. Head of Soviet state security Lavrentiy Beria proposed to Stalin that modernization of the backward Soviet economy proceed by seizing any German-owned plants located in Soviet-occupied Germany as war booty. Beria would create a special NKVD unit to secretly remove whole factories from the countries "liberated" from the German yoke and transplant them, along with their technically trained employees, to the Soviet Union.

In a rare expression of admiration for another person, Stalin pronounced it a brilliant idea and approved on the spot "Operation Kh." He ordered that it be given top priority. The designation "Kh" (X in Cyrillic) stood for the Russian word "khozyaystvo," meaning "economy," because it was an operation to revive the war-torn Soviet economy.

Within a few months, a new economic intelligence arm called "Line Kh" appeared in the Soviet foreign intelligence service and began frantically training officers in how to dismantle industrial plants for relocation. In 1944, when the Red Army left the Soviet borders behind it and marched westward, the INO began setting up "Kh rezidentury" (i.e., intelligence stations) in all the European countries that the Red Army had "liberated."

Beria's first success was Peenemünde, the German research center where Wernher von Braun and Walter Dornberger had designed the infamous V-2 rocket that terrorized London during the war. The Kh unit took everything home—Germans, equipment, blueprints, documents, and notes, then blew Peenemünde sky-high. Back in the Soviet Union, the military experts poring over their loot found that the V-2 wasn't even the best thing the Germans had invented. The Wasserfall (Waterfall), a surface-to-air missile, had been their latest technological invention, and its data enabled the Soviets to create their first long-range ballistic missile, the dreaded Scud.

After World War II, the Soviet Union suddenly had two commercially successful products exported to the West: photographic lenses and Pyrex glass. The technology, equipment, and experts to produce them had been stolen from German companies at the end of the war. One was the ZEISS optics and precision instruments firm, at that time the world's leading producer of lenses, microscopes, and photographic equipment. The other was the Schott glassworks, the world's largest supplier of Jenaer and Pyrex glass, a heat-resistant product invented by German chemist Friedrich Otto Schott and used in the manufacture of thermometers, cookware, and optical and chemical equipment.

Both companies had been located in Jena, and both were relocated to the Soviet Union by the INO's Kh unit. The operation was a dramatic race between Beria's unit, which was hurrying to dismantle the Jena optics industry, and the American Army, which was trying to preserve it. Working in a frenzy, the Americans were able to save some one hundred German scientists from the Jena optics and glass companies by hiding them in the American Zone.

In the end, however, the Soviets came out the winners. Through months of hard digging, the Kh unit was able to find many of the scientists and technicians in those two important industries and deport them to the Soviet Union. The Soviets also carried off most of the technical equipment from ZEISS and Schott. Both the machinery and the German technicians "proved to be worth more than their weight in gold," according to what Pacepa was later told.

Within a few years, the city of Jena was reborn in the Soviet Union. Prominently displayed in the Soviet wedding-cake-style city hall of the new town was the doctor's degree that in 1841 the University of Jena had awarded Karl Marx in absentia, a bonus discovered by Beria's officers in a musty old Jena archive.

Between 1922 and the German occupation of Romania in 1940, Pacepa's father managed the service department of the American General Motors company in Romania. From his father, Pacepa learned that the new Soviet automobile industry had been created in the same way. Stalin himself had given the name Pobeda (meaning victory) to the first Soviet passenger car built with equipment confiscated from General Motors, the manufacturer of Opel in Germany. GM was one of the largest American industrial firms in Germany. Before World War II it had produced more cars than any other European facility.

On the unforgettable day of October 24, 1959, Pacepa, who had just ended his term as chief of Romania's intelligence station in West Germany, arrived at his office earlier than usual to write his final report. That was not to be. An hour or so later, he was standing at attention in front of Alexandru Draghici, the minister of interior, who was just back from a meeting in Moscow, telling him that Khrushchev's new "technological revolution" had consumed everyone's attention there and that new KGB chairman "Comrade [Aleksandr Nikolayevich] Shelepin himself took the floor twice to address this subject." "Read this," Draghici ordered. It was an official appointment of Pacepa to chief of Romania's newly created department for technological intelligence, called S&T, from the Romanian *stiinta si technologie* (science and technology). In layman's terms: industrial espionage.

Pacepa's meeting with the minister of interior was not to be his last surprise that day. A baggy-panted KGB adviser was waiting for him at the DIE,[8] Romania's foreign intelligence service. "Privet," he greeted Pacepa tersely in Russian, giving him that typical KGB bone-crushing handshake. He then switched to fluent French. "I am Boris Alekseyevich, and I came from Moscow to introduce you in your new job." A chauffeur-driven Pobeda dropped both men at a lakeside villa in Snagov, a small weekend retreat township some thirty miles north of Bucharest.

"Believe me, Ivan Mikhaylovich, you're going to make history," Boris Alekseyevich said as soon as a maid had brought a generous supply of malossol caviar and vodka. The KGB adviser started his story back with Adam and Eve. "The period between the October Revolution of 1917 and the outbreak of World War II was an era when political considerations held sway in Soviet foreign intelligence." It was a time, Boris explained, when the Soviet leadership believed that communist ideology provided the key to everything, including the Soviet Union's industrialization. After the October Revolution, the Soviet Union had looted rich Russians, later the country's huge reserves of oil and gold, and after the war from Germany—he said with disarming frankness—from "you and your sister countries."

After the war, however, Stalin realized that he should pay attention to technological development as well, but he did so by pursuing technologies with potential military applications for nearly fifteen years. The KGB's Line Kh's military-technological intelligence thefts had lifted the Soviet Union to superpower status. In 1958 alone, the advisor said, over four thousand Soviet military equipment and weapons system research projects had benefited from Western hardware and technical documents obtained illegally by Line Kh. The budget for military technological intelligence and equipment theft included in the Soviet Union's sixth Five-Year Plan (1955–59) had risen to over 500 million dollars. It was estimated that in 1960, Line Kh would save the Soviet rocket industry alone roughly sixty-thousand man-years of scientific research. Nevertheless, it was unfortunate, the Soviet advisor added, that Stalin's vision had stopped there.

It had taken a Nikita Sergeyevich (Khrushchev) to discover Stalin's mistake, Boris Alekseyevich explained. Now Tovarishch Khrushchev had transformed Line Kh into a KGB directorate and ordered it to get involved in stealing domestic technologies from the West as well. That would be a piece of cake for us, Boris Alekseyevich thought, because while very important to the communist movement, most civilian technologies were not classified in the West. For the first time in history, the Soviet bloc would really be in a position to fulfill its historic destiny as the gravedigger of capitalism.

From his bottomless accordion briefcase, Boris Alekseyevich produced a volume that was almost as thick as a bible. "Here's your collection program for 1960," he explained. "It weighs more than Romania's whole foreign trade plan." As he flipped through the pages of his book, he commented that the largest iron and steel works in the world was going up near Novokuznetsk, as well as a huge oil refinery on the Amur River and a gigantic factory in Moldavia for tractors for orchards and vineyards. In his grand vision, industrial towers and chimneys had begun springing up over Russia's endless steppes like mushrooms after a summer rain, all guarded by endless rows of rockets boldly pointing their noses toward the West, and large underground factories building those rockets at the same rate that General Motors was manufacturing cars. "That's where Tovarishch Khrushchev's total technological espionage is going to take us."

The KGB colonel slammed his book shut and handed it to Pacepa. "You really should learn Russian," he said, exuding all the authority of the power behind the throne. "We have one big job to do, you and I." His pale blue eyes looked at Pacepa long and hard. "We are not here to record history, Ivan Mikhaylovich," he said. "We're here to make it!"

"Dogonyat i peregonyat!" Boris Alekseyevich closed solemnly, quoting Khrushchev's famous slogan about economically catching up with and overtaking the West in the space of ten years. "In the course of history, ten years is a mere second, isn't it?" Slapping the table in front of him, Boris Alekseyevich continued. "That is what Tovarishch Khrushchev told us after he got back from his long visit to America." There, he explained, Khrushchev had spent more time touring farms and factories than discussing politics with Eisenhower. Once back home, he had visited Directorate T. "We don't have time to reinvent the wheel. We've got to steal it!" he told us. "Don't raise your eyebrows, Comrades. I intentionally used the word steal. Stealing from capitalism is moral, Comrades." Boris Alekseyevich was now shouting and banging the table with true Khrushchev-like energy. "We must *steal* from capitalism!" the KGB colonel shouted once more, casting his voice in as close an imitation of Khrushchev's as he could manage.

Even today it is still a mystery to Pacepa why most of the Soviet advisors known to him took such pains to ape whatever Soviet leader happened to be in power at the moment. Under Stalin, they all wore military-style tunics buttoned to the neck, walked slowly, and spoke softly. Under Khrushchev, they switched to either ill-fitting clothes or raucous tones of voice. It was a Soviet peculiarity that Pacepa has never been able to explain. During Nicolae Ceausescu's long period in office, Romania succumbed to a cult of personality even more idiotic than Stalin's had been. But Pacepa never knew any Romanian who tried to stutter like Ceausescu.

CHAPTER 4

STEALING AMERICA'S NUCLEAR BOMB

Soon after World War II broke out, Joseph Stalin became worried that the world's big boys had bigger weapons than he did, so he set out to steal the Americans' nuclear bomb technology and famously succeeded. After becoming head of Romania's technological espionage service, Pacepa learned some of the details.

At first, Stalin tried to stay out of the fight by making a pact with Adolf Hitler, the most immediate threat. But Hitler double-crossed him by suddenly and without warning invading the Soviet Union on June 22, 1941, in Operation Barbarossa. The crisis pushed Stalin to consider the fact that the Americans had many brilliant Nobel Prize scientists working on game-changing weapons, while the Soviet Union had no scientists of that caliber. To catch up he set out to steal and copy the technology, ordering his chief intelligence official, Lavrentiy Beria, in mid-1941 to get cracking on the operation.

Beria assigned Vasily Zarubin—a senior intelligence officer then in New York and later the Washington, D.C. station chief—to the job. He passed the buck to Grigory Kheifetz, his talented station chief in San Francisco. Officially assigned to the Soviet Consulate there, Kheifetz was also known around town as "Mr. Brown" and had close working relationships with members of the American Communist Party (CPUSA). That fall of 1941, Kheifetz began hearing rumors that the United States Army was planning an atomic research laboratory in the nearby California desert and that Albert Einstein himself had told President Roosevelt he believed an atomic bomb was realistically feasible.

For Beria, however, Kheifetz's best news was that J. Robert Oppenheimer, a professor at the University of California at Berkeley, who was a longtime loyal although unlisted CPUSA member, was being considered for the job of scientific director. Moreover, Oppenheimer's wife was also a staunch communist and the widow of a communist political commissar who had died in the Spanish Civil War.

Does anyone now really still remember who J. Robert Oppenheimer was apart from being a brilliant California scientist who has been called the father of the atomic bomb of Hiroshima, which ended World War II? Wasn't there some kerfuffle over whether he was or wasn't a communist? Oppenheimer lost his clearance during the postwar hysteria over the many communists supposedly working in our government, but that all blew over, didn't it? Anyway, Oppenheimer helped us win the war, so he's an American hero, right?

An outstanding atomic physicist at the University of California at Berkeley, by late 1941 Oppenheimer was known to have been chosen by the U.S. Army to head a top-secret atomic research project. From September 1942 to November 1945, he was formally employed as the scientific director of the Manhattan Project's super-secret Radiation Laboratory located near Santa Fe, New Mexico. He oversaw its physical construction and personnel selection, brought about the first nuclear explosion test at Alamogordo on July 16, 1945, and is considered the father of the atomic bombs dropped on Japan that brought World War II to an official end on September 2, 1945. He returned to academia in November 1945.

At Berkeley, Oppenheimer was generally known to have communist leanings and in fact openly associated with communists. In early 1942, however, he inexplicably stopped attending Communist Party meetings or any political discussion groups or writing for communist publications. His colleagues believed he had experienced an honest change of heart due to his new responsibilities as an employee of the U.S. Army in wartime and as head of a laboratory performing secret work in support of the war effort. At this time he began counseling his left-leaning students not to get involved in Communist Party politics, and he dutifully reported to the Manhattan Project security office whenever party members tried to solicit his support for Russia.[1]

We coauthors do not buy that explanation. A sidebar here may illustrate the real story better than a technical digression on Soviet espionage and disinformation. For comparison purposes let's look at the true story recounted in the celebrated autobiography *Witness* by Whittaker Chambers, the one-time Soviet spy who later renounced communism and became a high-profile opponent.

Like Oppenheimer, Chambers was originally a dedicated communist, a talented man who as an agent could be of great use to Soviet intelligence. As editor of *The New Masses*—an official communist publication—Chambers was well known to local party members up and down the East Coast of the United States. One day in 1932, Max Bedacht, a member of the CPUSA's Central Committee (and secretly a liaison officer between the CPUSA and Soviet military intelligence), summoned Chambers to his office and announced: "They want you to go into one of the party's 'special institutions'... They want you to do underground work." He told Chambers he had to leave *The New Masses* and walk away from the open Communist Party. He also warned Chambers not to mention their conversation to anyone but his wife and told him to give him an answer the following day.

After talking it over with his wife that evening, Chambers decided not to do it because his wife was afraid and because he thought the people at his office would not understand why he was leaving. Unfortunately for him, when he went back to Bedacht the next day, the latter said: "You have no choice."

"He meant, of course," Chambers writes, "that I was under the discipline of the party and that, if I did not go into the underground, I would go out of the party" and be labeled a traitor. Bedacht immediately took him out for a walk and introduced him to "Don" from the "special institution." The latter told Chambers he could go to *The New Masses* one last time but never again. "In our work you will... never have anything to do with party people again. If you do, we will know it."[2]

Oppenheimer's behavior in early 1942 duplicates what Chambers was told to do, undoubtedly for the same reason. As an intelligence source, he was no longer allowed to associate openly with members of the CPUSA and was instructed to convince everyone in his daily life that he had turned his back on communism. Chambers, shortly after meeting the local party agent "Don," was introduced to an authoritative Russian who warned him that "henceforth I must absolutely separate myself from communists and the Communist Party, and live as much as possible like a respectable bourgeois."[3] That is just what Oppenheimer did.

Of course, when Chambers later decided to break with the party and the "underground" (in his case, Soviet military intelligence), he reacted entirely differently. In real fear for their lives, he and his family abruptly fled into total obscurity, only gradually daring to emerge into normal American life.[4] That is what Oppenheimer did not do.

Although Oppenheimer was obviously a very tempting target for recruitment by Soviet foreign intelligence, various disinformation sources later explained that because of his new assignment, he was so well guarded that it was difficult for Soviet assets to break through "the security cordon that surrounded him"[5] Or that Soviet military intelligence had made the first move and was already working on him.[6] All of this is pure eyewash, as will be seen later in our story.

Over the years, some of the most respected American researchers have studied Oppenheimer's case. The virtually unanimous conclusion has been that Oppenheimer was never a Soviet spy. In 2009 John Earl Haynes and Harvey Klehr published a book in which they flatly state that the available evidence is "of such quality and quantity that the case for Oppenheimer's innocence of the charge of assisting Soviet espionage is overwhelming: the case is closed."[7] Unfortunately, what is truly overwhelming is the barrage of disinformation the Russians have spread about Oppenheimer and the gullibility of educated Americans to believe it.

For the facts on Oppenheimer's activity as a spy for Soviet intelligence, we recommend *Special Tasks*, a remarkable memoir published in 1994 by Lt. Gen. Pavel Sudoplatov.[8] As a deputy chief of Soviet foreign intelligence, Sudoplatov was aware of the beginnings of the Oppenheimer case, although his own bailiwick was originally the Directorate of Special Tasks, the unsavory operations of which—"sabotage, kidnapping and assassination"—were carried out by illegal officers and agents completely divorced from the espionage being conducted by officers like Kheifetz.

Over the years, Sudoplatov has been unjustly maligned, primarily because his information does not fit with the universally accepted disinformation narrative that has been built around Oppenheimer and the bomb. Sudoplatov ran a tight little ship that didn't share personnel with other Soviet intelligence units and didn't leak. That was why Beria eventually put him in charge of atomic espionage activities at the Los Alamos Radiation Laboratory and why there exists virtually no independent confirmation of Sudoplatov's memoirs except in their own intrinsic logic and credibility. Beginning in 1943, Sudoplatov's illegals began playing a supporting role in handling the atomic intelligence received. Then in 1944, Beria put Sudoplatov directly in charge of a highly secret, new, and completely independent unit to handle the specific intelligence on the American atomic bomb that was being provided by Oppenheimer. Sudoplatov knew the facts because the Oppenheimer case was his responsibility.

Among Russian intelligence officers, Sudoplatov was initially praised for speaking out about his remarkable career, most notably for successfully organizing the 1940 assassination in Mexico of Stalin's main enemy, Leon Trotsky, without implicating the Soviet Union. After *Special Tasks* appeared in 1994, however, Russian officials wrote Sudoplatov off as a crazy old man, as did many Americans. In fact, Sudoplatov's memory was phenomenal. He made a strenuous effort to be accurate, having his son and his American coauthors, Jerrold and Leona Schecter, check out every detail wherever possible. He did not try to clear his book with Russian authorities, and he intended for it to be published in the United States, as it was. It rings absolutely true.

After hearing about Oppenheimer from Kheifetz, surely Beria could scarcely believe his luck. Kheifetz was clearly immediately instructed to find a way to meet Oppenheimer and try to win him over to helping the Soviet cause. In those days, the Soviet intelligence services (civilian, military, and party) had been happy to recruit agents from CPUSA members, knowing that they would be reliable sources and would follow instructions. Soon, however, Moscow realized that in foreign countries, identifiable party members attracted the attention of local police and security services, and since they all knew each other through party meetings, the arrest of one could compromise the whole group. Active agents who were party members were instructed to make a show of breaking with it.

Beginning in the 1950s, the intelligence services were in fact forbidden to recruit from among the members of foreign communist parties.

How could Lavrentiy Beria's foreign intelligence representatives in the United States manage to approach a brilliant scientist like Robert Oppenheimer in the ivory tower world of academia at the University of California at Berkeley? Even if he had been a longtime communist and therefore presumably friendly toward the Soviet Union, how could Oppenheimer be persuaded to engage in espionage in order to help the Soviet Union develop its own atomic bomb?

Sudoplatov's memoirs provide the only credible and recorded source to help us find an answer to these questions. He was directly involved on the Moscow end throughout the Oppenheimer case. Sudoplatov's memory of how the case developed not only makes perfect sense, it is a gripping story.[9]

Living in San Francisco at the time was a wealthy woman named Louise Brantsen, a paid CPUSA agent rumored to be Grigory Kheifetz's mistress. During the period 1936 to 1942, she threw soirées for people sympathetic to communist causes at her large house, where CPUSA members and Soviet intelligence officials could make interesting contacts.[10]

In late 1941, Vasily Zarubin, the Soviet foreign intelligence station chief in Washington, instructed Grigory Kheifetz, his very accomplished station chief in San Francisco, to find a way to approach Oppenheimer and obtain his cooperation. On December 6, 1941, Oppenheimer and his wife attended a cocktail party hosted by Louise Brantsen to raise money for Spanish Civil War veterans, which Kheifetz also attended. A personable Jew, he easily made friends with the Oppenheimers. He met them once again that month for cocktails, and by the end of December he managed to have a private lunch with Robert. That was when Oppenheimer agreed to cooperate with Soviet intelligence.[11]

It was surely not a coincidence that in January 1942, Robert Oppenheimer began renouncing all Communist Party connections.

Oppenheimer was the only person who would eventually have across-the-board access to all the Manhattan Project's scientific information and who understood its significance. According to Sudoplatov, Oppenheimer and his Manhattan Project close friends Enrico Fermi and Leon Szilard were afraid that the Nazis would produce the first atomic bomb. They believed that if the Americans shared their information with the Soviet Union, the Germans would be beaten to the bomb.

Beginning in 1942, Oppenheimer and his like-minded friends reported to the Soviets on the progress being made at the Manhattan Project orally, through comments and asides, and in documents clandestinely transferred "with their full knowledge that the information they were sharing would be passed on. In all, Oppenheimer sent five classified reports describing the progress of work on the atomic bomb."[12]

At the same time, however, Sudoplatov says the Manhattan Project scientists were treated as friends who cooperated with the Soviets but not as recruited agents. (In those days, becoming a Soviet "agent" was a formal step, with the agent signing his agreement to cooperate, receiving pay for his services, and being officially approved by Moscow. The atomic scientists were far too prominent to be asked to comply with any such bureaucratic procedures.)

From the beginning, extraordinary attention was paid to the security of the Oppenheimer operation. Vasily Zarubin, the Washington station chief, instructed Kheifetz to "divorce all intelligence operations" from the CPUSA, which was known to be "closely monitored by the FBI, and to have Oppenheimer sever all contacts with communists and left-wingers."[13]

In early 1942, Kheifetz introduced Oppenheimer's wife, Katherine, to the Washington station chief's wife, Elizabeth Zarubina—herself an intelligence officer with the rank of captain. Elizabeth began making frequent trips to California and building a close friendship with Katherine Oppenheimer. Kheifetz bowed out of the relationship, and from then on the contact ostensibly became a social connection between Elizabeth Oppenheimer and her close friend from out of town, who was unknown to the locals, including to the local FBI and CPSU.

Little by little, Sudoplatov's illegals began entering the picture. When he became head of Special Tasks in 1941, he made his old associate Leonid Eitingon his deputy. Eitingon, a principal organizer of Trotsky's assassination in 1940, was an old hand at illegal operations. During the period 1939 to 1941, he had recruited some forty unregistered illegal agents and planted them as sleepers around the U.S. and Mexico for possible use in sabotage operations. In 1941 he reactivated a dentist and his wife living in San Francisco, Polish Jews he had brought over from France in the 1930s. Eitingon introduced them to Zarubina, who introduced them to the Oppenheimers, and the couples began to socialize together. The Polish couple thereafter acted as couriers, passing Oppenheimer's documents at first to the Washington and New York foreign intelligence stations for forwarding to Moscow and later taking or sending them to Mexico City after the stations in the U.S. were, for increased security, cut out of the operation. Kheifetz and the Zarubinas were not only removed from the

Oppenheimer case, they were later recalled to Moscow for alleged transgressions—an in-house disinformation operation that we shall discuss later. A drugstore in Santa Fe, which had been used as a meeting point but was not compromised in the Trotsky assassination, became a safehouse where the Polish couple could also pass documents to other unregistered illegals. The latter would then act as couriers, taking the documents to Mexico City, where the Soviet intelligence station chief Lev Vasilievsky would receive them and ensure their clandestine transmission to Moscow.

This is only a sketchy summary of Sudoplatov's detailed account of how otherwise unknown assets and illegals left over from his previous "special tasks" operations were used to provide extreme security to the Oppenheimer operation and its intelligence product. Sudoplatov may not have had any scientific qualifications for his new job, but with his background in hush-hush dirty tricks and the whole apparatus that went with his specialty, he turned out to be a brilliant choice to handle atomic espionage.

In February 1944 Beria appointed Sudoplatov to be the director of a new, autonomous Department S "organized to supervise atomic intelligence activities of the GRU and the NKGB [state security]." At the same time, he was made head of the "Special Second Bureau of the newly set up State Committee for Problem Number One, whose aim was the realization of an atomic bomb through uranium fuel."[14]

On August 29, 1949, Soviet leader Joseph Stalin was in Moscow anxiously awaiting some very important news. Finally Lavrentiy Beria, his former state security chief and atomic espionage expert, called in from the Semipalatinsk test site in Kazakhstan to report that the Iosif-1 (the Soviet Union's first atomic bomb) had produced the exact same kind of mushroom cloud as in the American tests. With that news, Stalin found himself sitting on his very own cloud nine.

Coauthor Pacepa first heard the above story about Iosif-1 from the French physicist and prominent communist Frédéric Joliot-Curie when they were both in Geneva attending a United Nations Conference on the Peaceful Use of Atomic Energy. Joliot-Curie claimed to have been in Moscow at the time of the Iosif-1 test. A year later, Pacepa heard the same story from Igor Kurchatov, who headed the Soviet equivalent of the Manhattan Project and was attending a scientific meeting that the Romanians were hosting in Bucharest. Note that Stalin heard the good news about Iosif-1 from Beria, not from Kurchatov or from some military bigwig conducting the test. Iosif-1 was state security's bragging point.

CHAPTER 5

DISINFORMATION: THE ORIGINAL FAKE NEWS

isinformation, or "fake news," is not always a weapon used against an enemy. It can also be a corollary of the need-to-know principle observed by every intelligence service in wartime, inasmuch as "loose lips sink ships." Correspondingly, in the interest of victory in war, lies may be told. In the intelligence services we once managed, both coauthors observed misleading cables reporting that a recruitment attempt had failed, when in fact it had been a huge success; cable traffic on the real story had been moved to a very secure eyes-only channel to limit the number of officers aware of the case. Something similar happened in the Soviets' Oppenheimer case, although the measures taken were sometimes fairly drastic.[1]

By 1943, Moscow's foreign intelligence headquarters realized that too many of its officers who were under official cover and members of the CPUSA had been involved with the Oppenheimer case. It was true that the contact was now being handled more securely, thanks to Sudoplatov's experience running operations with illegal officers and agents, but conditions were still too insecure now that the FBI and Manhattan Project security were trying to identify communists hovering around American secrets.

Grigory Kheifetz was one officer whose CPUSA friendships and professional connections made him insecure. He had arranged to meet the Oppenheimers at the home of a paid CPUSA agent, Louise Brantsen.

Vasily Zarubin said that most of his U.S. recruitments had been based on CPUSA leads. His wife had been meeting with the Oppenheimers to receive documents for transmission to Moscow through official channels. Mexico City station chief Lev Vasilevsky also had past CPUSA connections and was now being given Oppenheimer materials from illegal couriers, or even from Zarubina, for transmission to Moscow by various means, including through the Washington and New York stations. These working relationships with the CPUSA were holdovers from the Comintern period, when the CPUSA had broken with Moscow and the intelligence services had temporarily bridged the gap. But that was no longer necessary. All of the above people were considered to be fine officers, but their close contacts with the CPUSA and their ingenious but unprofessional means of transmitting top security materials were by definition a worrisome security risk in the Oppenheimer case.

What did the bosses in Moscow do about it? In a nutshell, any officers involved in the Oppenheimer case who might in any way attract the attention of official American authorities or of CPUSA members were simply recalled to Moscow, mostly "in disgrace." Some were reportedly rehabilitated, some allegedly killed (but the last fate was presumably disinformation). By February 1944, Sudoplatov had taken the Oppenheimer case securely under his belt in his new and autonomous Department S, where it was handled exclusively by illegal officers and agents with no connection to anything or anyone else.

Grigory Kheifetz was recalled to Moscow in July 1944. Sudoplatov reports only that thereafter, Kheifetz became involved with Jewish affairs, for which he was eventually arrested and ended up in a prison hospital.[2] Kheifetz is not even mentioned in the voluminous Mitrokhin Archive, a reliable source consisting of documents in the KGB's normal foreign directorate archive that were smuggled out to England in 1993 by the defector Vasili Mitrokhin.[3] The spurious Vassiliev notebooks, on the other hand, which the KGB officially released for publication in the U.S. in 2009, contain voluminous references to Kheifetz, his recall for "failing to cope with his job," and even his alleged written report defending his failure to recruit Oppenheimer because the Communist Party of the Soviet Union did not come through with its plans to introduce him and because the GRU was working on Oppenheimer and had failed to turn him over to the KGB. The American editors of the Vassiliev notebooks firmly dismiss all of Sudoplatov's reporting on atomic espionage as the ramblings of a weak mind based on "sparse documentation with no provenance."[4]

Vasily Zarubin and his wife, Yelizaveta, were also recalled to Moscow in mid-1944. According to Sudoplatov, one of Zarubin's subordinates in the United States, Lt. Col. Vasily Mironov, had denounced Zarubin for having been careless in meeting American agents and accused him of being a double agent for the FBI in a letter to Stalin. The investigation against Zarubin "lasted six months and established that he was not working with the FBI," but in 1946 he was fired with the rank of general.[5] The Mitrokhin Archive records Mironov's letter was sent anonymously to J. Edgar Hoover, head of the FBI, and dates it August 7, 1943. The letter reportedly identifies ten other intelligence officers, including Mironov himself, working under diplomatic cover in the United States. Mironov also accused Zarubin of being a spy for Japan and accused his wife of working for the Germans. Another Mironov letter to Stalin accused Zarubin of being in contact with the FBI. In the summer of 1944, both Zarubins and Mironov were recalled to Moscow. Zarubin quickly established his position in Moscow and was appointed deputy chief of foreign intelligence, which was not good for Mironov. Zarubin retired three years later, allegedly for ill health, while "taking much of the credit for the remarkable wartime intelligence obtained from the United States" and was awarded two Orders of Lenin, two Orders of the Red Banner, one Order of the Red Star, and numerous other medals. His success in the United States is attributed to his having worked closely with the CPUSA.[6] Regarding Mironov's letters denouncing the Zarubins, Vasiliev's notebooks say that the Zarubins were recalled, investigated, and cleared and that Mironov was demoted, sent to a labor camp, and executed in 1945 for trying to smuggle a letter out to the U.S. embassy.[7] Sudoplatov says Mironov was recalled and arrested but then diagnosed as schizophrenic, hospitalized, and discharged from the service.[8]

We coauthors suspect, though we cannot prove, that the contradictory "Mironov affair" may have been part of an effort by state security leaders to clear the decks in the United States. From Central Committee CPSU archives, Sudoplatov's American coauthors, Jerrold and Leona Schecter, later learned that Kheifetz was promoted to lieutenant colonel of State Security on December 15, 1944, and that Zarubina was promoted to the same position on December 22, 1945.[9]

Lev Vasilevsky, foreign intelligence station chief in Mexico City at the time of the Oppenheimer operation, met with illegal couriers, Zarubin's wife, and officers at the Washington and New York stations as part of the improved if still risky chain to move the "take" from Oppenheimer to Moscow. According to the Mitrokhin Archive, in August 1944 Lev Tarasov (Vasilevsky's cover name in Mexico City) was denounced by Kheifetz for having bungled his part in the Trotsky operation and for spending too much time on his house and birds in Mexico instead of working. He was recalled.[10] According to Sudoplatov, Vasilevsky was then briefly deputy chief of Sudoplatov's Department S. Arrested in 1948 in connection with the anti-Semitic purges, he was nevertheless permitted to retire on salary. He died in 1949.[11] According to the Vassiliev notebooks, around October 1945 in Moscow, Vasilevsky drew up a plan of action for Boris Merkulov, head of state security, approved by Pavel Fitin, head of foreign intelligence, that said more case officers were needed in the western USA to work on the atomic bomb target because so far nothing had been done on that. He suggested setting up a "new operations center on the West Coast that would focus on work at the University of California," specifically listing three targets for technical intelligence: "Ernest Lawrence and the still elusive Oppenheimer brothers."[12] (Robert's brother Frank was also a communist and professor at Berkeley.)

The above contradictory stories leave us with certain obvious conclusions. Sudoplatov was on the scene to know the truth, and his memoirs were never censored by Moscow, so he is credible. Mitrokhin knows what foreign intelligence officers were told. He wasn't censored by Moscow either, but he was not personally involved with the Oppenheimer case, so he reflects the "in-house" disinformation spread among uninvolved foreign intelligence officers so as to make the Oppenheimer case known only those with a "need to know." The Vassiliev notebooks are not credible, because they were created by the KGB specifically for publication in the United States and surfaced shortly after the publication of Sudoplatov's memoirs. Its many references to the unrecruited Robert Oppenheimer appear to us to be disinformation designed to conceal the fact that he was actually a cooperative source who enabled Russia to build its own atomic bomb.

General Pavel Sudoplatov died peacefully in Moscow on September 26, 1996, but his campaign to expose the truth about Russia has been carried on by his American coauthors, Jerrold and Leona Schecter. In 2003, the

Schecters published a book of their own entitled *Sacred Secrets*, based on newly released documents from Russian and American archives. Included is one fascinating letter that lends support to our conclusions about the Oppenheimer case.[13]

This letter is dated October 2, 1944, is classified TOP SECRET and UR-GENT by Boris Merkulov, the head of state security, to his boss, Lavrentiy Beria, the commissar for internal affairs. The Schecters reproduce a photograph of the original Russian letter and their English translation. The typed letter contains underlined blanks that have been filled in by hand, evidently as a security measure. This is copy number two of three, apparently Merkulov's copy that had been returned to him signed with Beria's approval.

The Schecters do not state how they obtained the photograph of this letter, but from its contents, we coauthors believe the letter to be genuine. Merkulov writes:

In accordance with your instruction of September 29, 1944, the NKGB USSR is continuing measures for obtaining more complete information on the status of work on the problem of uranium and its development abroad.

In the period 1941-1943, important data on the start of research and work in the USA on this problem was received from our foreign agent network using the contacts of Comrades Zarubin and Kheifetz in their execution of important tasks in line with the executive committee of the Comintern.

In 1942, one of the leaders of scientific work on uranium in the USA, Professor Oppenheimer, an unlisted member of the apparat of Comrade Browder, informed us about the start of work.

At the request of Comrade Kheifetz, confirmed by Comrade Browder, he provided cooperation in access to the research for several of our tested sources, including a relative of Comrade Browder.

Due to complications of the operational situation in the USA, the disso-lution of the Comintern, and the explanations of Comrades Zarubin and Kheifets on the Mironov affair, it seems expedient to immediately sever the contacts of leaders and activists of the CPUSA with scientists and specialists engaged in work on uranium.

The NKGB requests to obtain the agreement of the leadership.

This copy of the letter is not the one Merkulov signed and sent off; it is the copy he got back, signed and approved by Beria and dated October 2, 1944. Merkulov notes at the top that he received Beria's agreement on October 3, 1944.

During the summer of 1944, Merkulov had cleaned house in his U.S. stations. One way or another, all the officers who had been on friendly working terms with Earl Browder and his CPUSA had been sent home to Moscow. The "uranium" project, as Merkulov called the atomic bomb research, was by the time of Merkulov's letter already in Sudoplatov's competent, tightly clenched fists and did not need any help from the CPUSA. Oppenheimer and his friends were providing the best intelligence possible on the atomic bomb, and any contacts with CPUSA members such as Browder's relative only endangered the really valuable sources.

It is noteworthy that in this letter, Merkulov flatly stated that in 1942 Oppenheimer "informed us" about the start of work on the Manhattan Project. "Us" was clearly Soviet state security, not the CPSU. The two state security officers in direct touch with Oppenheimer in 1942 were Grigory Kheifetz and Elizabeth Zarubina. They had done an outstanding job working with Oppenheimer, but in the summer of 1944 they had been abruptly recalled to Moscow for what proved to be completely false accusations. The real reason they were recalled, along with Zarubina's husband, was their prior close cooperation with the CPUSA. The above letter shows that Merkulov recognized a potentially serious threat to the security of his extremely valuable Oppenheimer case inherent in any connections with the CPUSA.

Beria understood the problem. That was why he had put Sudoplatov in charge of the whole atomic bomb operation in the first place. According to Sudoplatov, in January 1945 the Soviets would receive a description of the design of the first atomic bomb.[14]

Moscow never publicly acknowledged that Robert Oppenheimer had helped the KGB steal the technology of the nuclear bombs and build Iosif-1. It feared that any publicity around Oppenheimer would deter other potential American sources from helping the KGB keep in step with American nuclear progress on this, the weaponry of the future. The 1985 redefection from the U.S. of KGB Colonel Vitaly Yurchenko proved the KGB right. After twenty-five years of serving the KGB, Yurchenko did what General Pacepa had done a few years earlier—he requested political asylum in the U.S. during an assignment abroad in the summer of 1985. As had Pacepa, Yurchenko asked the CIA to keep his defection a secret. Yurchenko had also left a child behind, and he was afraid that Western publicity about his defection could make his child's life a hell.

Unfortunately, a few months later, Yurchenko's defection became front page news in the U.S. Also unfortunately, one of the CIA's debriefers of Yurchenko was Aldrich Ames, who in 1993 was sentenced to life in prison without parole for being a paid Soviet spy. During a dinner at Au Pied de Cochon, a restaurant in the Georgetown section of Washington, D.C., in November 1985, Yurchenko told his CIA guard, "I'm going for a walk. If I don't come back, it is not your fault." Yurchenko never returned. Several days later the Soviet embassy in Washington called a press conference, at which Yurchenko told the media that he had not defected to the CIA. He had been drugged and kidnapped by the CIA. It was, of course, a lie, but that press conference was followed by a virulent *dezinformatsiya* campaign aimed at transforming that lie into truth. It seemed that the whole Soviet bloc intelligence machinery—almost a million officers—did nothing during those days but pour vitriol on the CIA, which was painted as the most evil of evils. To a professional intelligence officer, that grotesque KGB portrait of the CIA looked like an unsavory cartoon. Unfortunately, it put down roots within American public opinion and became "the truth."

In 1986, Director of Central Intelligence Bill Casey sent General Pacepa a letter explaining the failure that had led to Yurchenko's redefection. "The root cause," Casey explained, was the CIA's inability to keep Yurchenko's defection a secret.[15] That was indeed true. But it was also manna from heaven for the KGB, which launched a disinformation campaign aimed at persuading the media and America's main Sovietologists into believing that the real "traitor" was not in the KGB but rather in the White House: Harry Hopkins, the closest confidant of President Franklin D. Roosevelt.

During his relatively short debriefings by the CIA, Yurchenko, who had once been chief of the KGB station in Washington, identified the KGB's most important agents in the Washington area that he knew of: Ronald William Pelton at the NSA and Edward Lee Howard at the CIA. Both were arrested by the FBI and sentenced for espionage. Yurchenko never mentioned Hopkins, to the best of our knowledge, yet as chief of the KGB station in Washington, Yurchenko should have been aware of Hopkins had he been a Soviet agent, and revealing him would have greatly increased Yurchenko's standing in the U.S. Hopkins lived in the White House during the last years of his life. To the best of our combined knowledge, the KGB never had any agent there. President Roosevelt did everything in his power to extend the life of Hopkins, who suffered from an aggressive intestinal cancer.

Yet suddenly, after the Yurchenko redefection, Hopkins was suspected everywhere of having been a Soviet spy. The evidence to support that accusation is weak, but as Chairman Mao once said, a lie repeated a hundred times becomes the truth.

In the 1930s and early 1940s, Soviet foreign intelligence in the U.S. had loose security in both its legal and illegal stations. Quite a few important Soviet agents were compromised, and their names were published. Hopkins was not among them. In September 1945, when a military code clerk, Igor Gouzenko, defected in Ottawa, Soviet state security boss Lavrentiy Beria realized how lax security had been. On April 7, 1946, he therefore issued a book cable to all his stations abroad, saying that "the most elementary rules of conspiracy were being ignored" and telling the stations to pay special attention to tightening security.[16] Again, Hopkins was never mentioned. KGB General Sudoplatov, who in the late 1980s exposed all the high-ranking Americans who had collaborated with Soviet intelligence in the nuclear field, didn't mention him either. As we read the totality of the evidence, Hopkins was not a Soviet agent.

In a way, the study of espionage is like the study of fine art; the more you know about it, the easier it is to spot a fake. In espionage, the art of forgery is called disinformation. After World War II, American and European leftists needed a new enemy, and the Kremlin's *dezinformatsiya* machinery obliged. President Truman was painted as the "butcher of Hiroshima," Eisenhower as a war-mongering "shark" run by the military-industrial complex, Johnson as a mafia boss who had bumped off his predecessor, Nixon as a petty tyrant, Ford as a dimwitted football player, Jimmy Carter as a bumbling peanut farmer, and Ronald Reagan as a third-class Hollywood actor.

The case of Harry Hopkins, one of President Franklin Roosevelt's most trusted advisers during World War II, was added by Moscow on this list of forgeries in 1985. The specific allegations that Hopkins was a Soviet spy lie in KGB General Yurchenko's 1985 post-redefection statements, when he publicly lied, telling the U.S. media that he had in fact never defected to the CIA but had been kidnapped by the CIA, and in a 1985 report from Oleg Gordievsky, one of the most knowledgeable defectors from the KGB.

We do not trust Yurchenko, who during the same year of 1985 redefected to communist Moscow, but we have high confidence in Gordievsky. The problem is that Gordievsky learned about the so-called KGB recruitment of Hopkins under dubious conditions and from dubious sources. In about 1964, while working in the illegals directorate of the KGB, Gordievsky heard a lecture at the Lubyanka headquarters in Moscow given by Iskhak Akhmerov, a former illegal KGB officer in Washington, D.C. Akhmerov devoted most of his lecture to his relations with Harry Hopkins, whom he described as "the most important of all Soviet wartime agents in the United States." Akhmerov was evidently an impressive speaker, going into great detail about how he had handled Hopkins over the years, passing him personal wishes from Stalin and molding Hopkins into a hugely valuable agent.[17]

This story simply does not add up. There is no factual basis for assuming that Akhmerov even met Hopkins, much less that he handled him as an agent. We know that after his retirement Akhmerov used to give lectures for the illegals directorate, but we also know it was against all KGB rules to discuss real cases by true names or in any identifiable way. On the other hand, it was quite common to embellish lectures for educational purposes, improving on the true scenario. In other words, we have no reason to question what Gordievsky remembers about Akhmerov's lecture, but we believe Akhmerov's whole story was cleverly delivered disinformation designed to inspire its listeners. Furthermore, we have found no other source—including defectors and electronic intercepts— that suggests any contact between Hopkins and Akhmerov.

The portrait of Hopkins in Akhmerov's lecture was certainly a forgery, just as the KGB and FSB portraits of all post–World War II American presidents were forgeries. Akhmerov's whole life was a forgery. The basic skeleton of his Hopkins story might have been drawn from the case of Lawrence Duggan, a rising State Department star recruited and handled by Akhmerov himself. Later, Akhmerov also handled Michael Straight, a wealthy young American recruited in England by one of the famous Cambridge spies who in 1938 returned to the United States, where Eleanor Roosevelt helped him get a job at the State Department. There is, however, no factual basis for assuming that Akhmerov ever even met Hopkins, much less that he ever handled him as an agent.

During the war, Gen. Sudoplatov headed the illegals directorate that became Directorate S of the First (foreign intelligence) Chief Directorate (PGU) upon Stalin's death. (In fact it was named Directorate S in honor of Sudoplatov.) In his memoirs, published in 1994, he describes all agents recruited by his service in the West, but he makes no mention of any contact between Hopkins and Akhmerov.

Hopkins's public and friendly contacts with many Soviet officials, including Stalin himself, may sound sinister today, but it must be remembered that the Soviets were our wartime allies, President Roosevelt encouraged those contacts, and it was Hopkins's job to be nice to the Soviets so they would help us win the war. If Hopkins really were a clandestine Soviet agent, its foreign intelligence service would have insisted he not call attention to himself by socializing with Soviet officials or expressing the pro-Soviet sentiments that he did. That was the rule.

In short, Oleg Gordievsky did not misremember, but Akhmerov's portrait of Harry Hopkins was probably a forgery. Now Lt. General Michael Flynn, President Trump's former chief of staff, is being accused of being a Russian spy because he had spoken on the phone with the Russian ambassador in the U.S.

DEVELOPING THE SECRET INK

For fifty-seven years we have had irrefutable intelligence evidence showing that Nikita Khrushchev and his political police were involved in the assassination of President John F. Kennedy. This overwhelming evidence was posted in the twenty-six volumes of *The President's Commission on the Assassination of President Kennedy*, but few, if any, have been able to understand its significance. The reason? This evidence, which is codified, has never before been jointly analyzed by a top U.S. intelligence leader and a former Soviet bloc spy chief familiar with KGB patterns and codes. It took us years to do this, but the results are illuminating.

Decoded, these pieces of evidence prove that John F. Kennedy's assassin, Lee Harvey Oswald, had a clandestine meeting in Mexico City with his Soviet case officer, "comrade Kostin," who has been identified by the CIA as belonging to the KGB's Thirteenth Department for assassinations abroad. It also proves that Oswald's wife, Marina, came to the United States using a false Soviet birth certificate and that both Oswalds fully intended to return to the Soviet Union after Lee had accomplished his KGB mission. A letter from Marina and Lee to the Soviet embassy in Washington is irrefutable proof of that.

Decoded, this evidence also proves that Oswald's KGB support officer in the United States, the so-called American named Baron George de Mohrenschildt (who had changed his biography three times), was in fact a Soviet illegal officer. It also documents that de Mohrenschildt committed suicide the day before he was scheduled to testify about Oswald to Congress and that he left behind a manuscript dedicated to Nikita Khrushchev, the last Soviet leader to whom he would have sworn allegiance as a KGB illegal officer.

Here is a graphic sample of such evidence we put together. Each piece of this evidence was published in the Warren Commission Report, and each piece has been declassified to restore "public confidence in government" and allow the American public to "draw its own conclusion as to what happened and why on that fateful day in Dallas in November 1963."[†]

There are hundreds more such similar pieces of irrefutable hard evidence buried in the investigative documents concerning the assassination of President Kennedy and waiting to be exposed. They can be found and read, free of charge, in most public libraries. Let's hope this book will bring them to life again.

† Final Report of the Assassination Records Review, https://fas.org/sgp/advisory/arrb98/part12htm.

MORE SECRET WRITING

Intelligence operations are usually written in secret ink, and they cannot be read unless one has the developer. Properly developed, the available intelligence documents produced by or for Lee Harvey Oswald prove that he was an agent of Soviet foreign intelligence and that he was trained for political assassination.

SYNOPSIS

The PGU recruited Oswald in 1957 while he was serving as a Marine in Japan. Brought "black" to Moscow in 1959 to be debriefed and readied for a new intelligence assignment in Europe, Oswald provided information that enabled the Soviets—for the first and last time—to shoot down an American U-2 spy plane on May Day in 1960. Although Oswald wished to remain in the Soviet Union, and his assignment to Europe was canceled, he was eventually persuaded to return to the U.S. on a temporary mission to assassinate President Kennedy, whom Khrushchev had come to despise. Oswald was taken over by the PGU (the first chief directorate of the KGB) component for assassinations abroad (Thirteenth Department), given a Soviet wife, and sent back to the U.S. in June 1962.

The Thirteenth Department also dispatched Oswald's case officer (Valery Kostikov, alias Kostin) as a diplomat at the Soviet embassy in Mexico City to be available for secret meetings with Oswald. At that time, Mexico was the most desirable place for contacts with the bloc's important agents in the U.S. *Operation Dragon* documents that Oswald and Kostikov met there at least once and probably twice. In the fall of 1962, however, a public trial in West Germany accused Khrushchev of personally ordering two political killings there, and all foreign assassinations throughout the Soviet bloc were called off. The PGU repeatedly tried but was unable to dissuade the obstinate Oswald from carrying out his mission. Using the tradecraft the PGU had taught him, Oswald went ahead on his own, believing that afterward he could return to a hero's welcome in Moscow.

In order to prove to the PGU that he could pull off an assassination undetected, Oswald tried and just barely failed to kill American General Edwin Walker, but the PGU still gave him the cold shoulder at a secret meeting in Mexico City. His support officer in the U.S., George de Mohrenschildt, was immediately pulled off the case and moved to Haiti. Contingency plans were initiated for silencing Oswald should he commit the unthinkable. At a second meeting in Mexico City a few months later, "Comrade Kostin" again failed to deprogram the fanatical Oswald.

On November 22, 1963, Oswald succeeded in killing President Kennedy without PGU help or blessing, and two days later Oswald himself was killed by Jack Ruby, as arranged by the PGU with Cuban help. When Ruby was about to be released from jail in 1967, the PGU apparently had him killed by cancer-causing radiation.

As long-time PGU chief Sakharovsky often said, dead men cannot tell tales.

DEVELOPING THE
SECRET INK

CONVENTIONAL WISDOM :   Moscow had no secret connection with Oswald.

FACT :   Oswald used PGU operational codes even in correspondence with his Soviet wife, Marina.

DOCUMENTARY EVIDENCE :   The "Walker Note." Oswald left this very important note for Marina on April 10, 1963, just before shooting at, and barely missing, U.S. General Edwin Walker. The Walker Note contains two PGU operational codes: friends (code for support officer) and Red Cross (code for financial help). In this handwritten note, in Russian, Oswald tells Marina what to do in case he is arrested. He stresses that she should contact the (Soviet) embassy, that they have "friends here," and that the "Red Cross" will help her financially.

Particularly significant is Oswald's instruction for her to "send the embassy the information about what happened to me." At that time the code for embassy was "office," but it seems that Oswald wanted to be sure Marina would understand she should immediately inform the Soviet embassy. It is noteworthy that Marina did not mention this note to the U. S. authorities after Oswald's arrest. It was found at the home of Ruth Paine, with whom Marina was staying at the time of the assassination.

Original text, in Russian, of the "Walker Note" (pg. 1).

NOTE. Ciphers and codes are the most sensitive aspects of any foreign intelligence service. For the last ten years of General Pacepa's communist career, he supervised Romania's counterpart of the American NSA, thus becoming familiar with Soviet patterns for ciphers and codes.

DEVELOPING THE
SECRET INK

HERE IS THE ENGLISH TRANSLATION OF THE "Walker Note," WITH EMPHASIS AS IN THE ORIGINAL.

1. This is the KEY to the mailbox of the main post office, found in the city, on ERVAY street the same street where the drugstore is where you always stood. 4 blocks from the drugstore on the same street to the post office there you will find our box. I paid for the box last month so don't worry about it.

2. Send the embassy the information about what happened to me and also clip from the newspaper, (if anything is written about me in the paper) I think the embassy will quickly help you when it knows everything.

3. I paid for the house on the 2nd so don't worry about that.

4. I also paid for the water and gas not long ago.

5. It is possible there will be money from work, they will send to our box at the post office. Go to the bank and change the check into cash.

6. My clothes etc. you can throw out or give away. Do not keep them. But my PERSONAL papers (military, factory, etc.) I prefer that you keep.

7. A few of my documents are in the blue small valise.

8. The address book is on my table in the study, if you need it.

9. We have friends here and the Red Cross will also help you. (Red Cross [sic] in English)

10. I left you money as much as I could, 60$ on the 2nd, and you and June can live on 10$ a week. 2 months more.

11. If I am alive and they have taken me prisoner, the city jail is located at the end of that bridge that we always rode over when we went into town. (the very beginning of the city after the bridge.)

DEVELOPING THE SECRET INK

CONVENTIONAL WISDOM :   Oswald had no ties with the Thirteenth Department of the PGU charged with assassinations abroad.

FACT :   A few weeks before killing President Kennedy, Oswald secretly met *his Thirteenth Department case officer*, Valery Kostikov, alias "Kostin," in Mexico City.

DOCUMENTARY EVIDENCE :   Oswald's letter to the Soviet embassy in Washington, D.C., dated November 9, 1963, and a first draft found at Paine's house. This is another very important letter, which Oswald wrote after returning from his second trip to Mexico City. In it, **he states that he traveled to Mexico City under a different name** and that **he met "Comrade Kostin"** there.

Other evidence is in the free guidebook *Esta Semana* (*This Week*), which Oswald brought back from his September–October 1963 trip to Mexico City. Next to the list of embassies, he wrote the names "**KOSTEN**" and "**OSVALD**" in Cyrillic. Furthermore, while in Mexico City, on October 1, 1963, Oswald spoke by telephone from the Cuban embassy with a guard at the Soviet embassy (a conversation intercepted by the CIA) to ask about his Soviet visa, which Oswald said **he had discussed with "Comrade Kostikov."** Valery Kostikov, alias Kostin, was an identified PGU officer of the Thirteenth Department who was assigned under consular cover to the Soviet embassy in Mexico shortly before Oswald repatriated from the Soviet Union.

Photocopy of Oswald's November 9, 1963, letter.

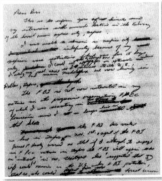

Draft of the same letter, found in Ruth Paine's garage.

DEVELOPING THE
SECRET INK

Esta Semana – Cover.

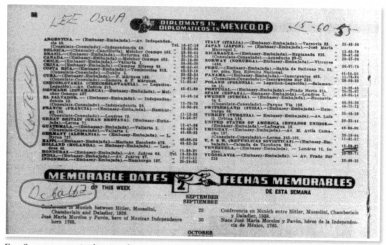

Esta Semana, page 2, showing the names KOSTEN and OSVALD in Cyrillic.

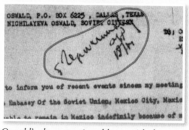

Oswald's above mentioned letter with the name **Gerasimov** *enlarged.*

NOTE. Although addressed to Soviet Consul Reznichenko (whose name Oswald had in his wallet even on the day he was arrested), the letter can be seen to have been signed off on at the top of the page by Vitaly Gerasimov. He was an identified PGU officer assigned under diplomatic cover in the U.S., whose signature appears on most of the Oswalds' correspondence with the Soviet embassy in Washington. (These letters were furnished to the U.S. by the Soviet government.)

DEVELOPING THE SECRET INK

HERE IS THE FINAL LETTER IN ENGLISH, WITH THE EARLIER DRAFT VERSION INDICATED IN BRACKETS.

FROM: LEE H. OSWALD, P.O. BOX 6225, DALLAS, TEXAS
MARINA NICHILAYEVA OSWALD, SOVIET CITIZEN

TO: CONSULAR DIVISION
EMBASSY U.S.S.R
WASHINGTON, D.C.
NOV, 9, 1963

Dear sirs;
This is to inform you of recent events since my meetings with comrade Kostin *[in draft: "of new events since my interviews with comrade Kostine"]* in the Embassy of the Soviet Union, Mexico City, Mexico. I was unable to remain in Mexico *[crossed out in draft: "because I considered useless"]* indefinily because of my mexican visa restrictions which was for 15 days only. I could not take a chance on reqesting a new visa *[in draft: "applying for an extension"]* unless I used my real name, so I retured to the United States. *[In draft: "I and Marina Nicholeyeva are now living in Dallas, Texas, you already ha"—last three words crossed out.]*
[In draft, paragraph about FBI is located here.]
I had not planned to contact the Soviet embassy in Mexico so they were unprepared, *[in draft: "It was unfortunate that the Soviet Embassy was unable to aid me in Mexico City, but I had not planned to contact the Mexico City Embassy at all so of course they were unprepared for me."]* had I been able to reach the Soviet Embassy in Havana as planned, the embassy there would have had time to complete our business. *[Crossed out in draft after planned: "I could have contacted the Soviet Embassy there for the completion of— would have been able to help me—assist me—get the necessary documents as I required." Not crossed out in draft: "would have had time to assist me, but of course the stuip Cuban Consule was at fault here, I'm glad he has since been replaced by another.]*
Of corse the Soviet embassy was not at fault, they were, as I say unprepared, the Cuban consulate was guilty of a gross breach of regulations, I am glad he has since been replced.
The Federal Bureau of Investigation is not now interested in my activities in the progressive organization "Fair Play for Cuba Committee", of which I was secretary in New Orleans (state Louisiana) since I no longer reside in *[crossed out: "am no longer connected with"]* that state. However, the F.B.I. has visted us here in Dallas, Texas, on November 1st. Agent James P. Hasty warned me that if I engaged *[in draft: "attempt to engage"]* in F.P.C.C. activities in Texas the F.B.I. will again take an "interrest" in me. This agent also "suggested" to Marina Nichilayeva that she could remain in the United States under F.B.I. "protection", that is, she could defect from *[in draft: "refuse to return to"]* the Soviet Uion, of couse, I and my wife strongly protested these tactics by the notorious F.B.I..
Please inform us of the arrival of our Soviet entrance visa's as soon as they come.
Also, this is to inform you of the birth, on October 20, 1963, of a DAUGHTER, AUDREY MARINA OSWALD in DALLAS, TEXAS, to my wife.

Respectfully,
[s] Lee H. Oswald

NOTE. Letter written with Oswald's original misspellings.

DEVELOPING THE SECRET INK

CONVENTIONAL WISDOM : Oswald had no direct contact with the PGU during his years in the Soviet Union.

FACT : There are valid indications that the PGU trained Oswald in the techniques of clandestine communications.

DOCUMENTARY EVIDENCE : The word microdot written by Oswald in his address book next to the entry for Jaggars-Chiles-Stovall, a Dallas graphics firm

whose photocopying equipment was used by Oswald to fabricate false identity documents for himself. There Oswald once explained to a fellow employee (Denis Ofstein, retired U.S. Army, security branch) that microdots are used in espionage to secretly transmit documents reduced to a dot and hidden "under a postage stamp." In the 1960s, microdots were all the rage in the PGU (and the DIE).

Photocopy of Oswald's address book page containing the word microdot.

Hiding them under a postage stamp was the favorite microdot technique at that time and also one of the best-kept secrets in the Soviet bloc intelligence community.

After returning to the U.S., Oswald occasionally listed his occupation as "photographer," although he is not known ever to have been overtly trained as one. On September 17, 1963, for instance, he listed his occupation as photographer when applying for a Mexican tourist card. The PGU (and the DIE) went to great lengths to give their agents photographic training.

U.S. Secret Service Report stating that Oswald listed his profession as "photographer."

DEVELOPING THE
SECRET INK

CONVENTIONAL WISDOM :   There were no clandestine
communications between the PGU
and Oswald in the U.S.

FACT :   Oswald was at least trained to be ready
for a clandestine communications
system with the PGU.

DOCUMENTARY EVIDENCE :   Marina Oswald's Russian housekeeping
guide, *Kniga poleznykh sovetov* (*Book of Useful Advice*), described in Warren
Commission documents as containing 865 pages, the first eighteen of which were
missing. No innocuous explanation has been found for these missing pages—would
an American housewife mutilate her *Joy of Cooking* that way in a foreign country
where she could not replace it?

There is an operational reason for the missing pages, however. In the 1960s, it
was common practice for the Thirteenth Department (and for the DIE equivalent,
Group Z) to give its important agents some large inoffensive book, a duplicate of
which was kept by headquarters, to use for encrypting or decrypting messages sent
as microdots or secret writing. The agent had to tear out each page once used to
be sure not to reuse it.

The book page autographed by Oswald.

The *Book of Useful
Advice* is inscribed: "July
12, 1961, from Lee to
Marina." Two days earlier
Oswald had gotten back
his American passport
from the U.S. embassy in
Moscow and requested a
visa for Marina's travel to
the U.S. Now the PGU
was, evidently, sure that
Oswald could return to
the U.S. and could therefore be equipped with the materials he would need for
conducting clandestine communications with the Thirteenth Department. Marina
did not tell the authorities about her *Book of Useful Advice*, but it clearly was
significant to her as that was where she kept the previously mentioned "Walker
Note" telling her what to do if Oswald should be arrested.

DEVELOPING THE SECRET INK

CONVENTIONAL WISDOM :   After spending two years in the Soviet Union, Oswald soured on Soviet communism and in 1962 returned to the U.S. for good.

FACT :   Oswald considered himself on a *temporary mission* in the U.S., and he was determined to return to the Soviet Union after accomplishing it.

DOCUMENTARY EVIDENCE :   Letters of July 1, 1963, asking the Soviet embassy in Washington, D.C., to grant an entrance visa for Marina and another one "separtably" (misspelling in original text) for Oswald. It is clear that Oswald wanted to see his wife and children back in the Soviet Union before assassinating President Kennedy and that he required a **separate entry visa** for himself to be able to disappear into the inscrutable Soviet Union after accomplishing his mission.

Photocopy of Marina's letter, in Russian, with Oswald's attached note in English.

In fact, soon after returning to the U.S. in 1962, Oswald asked the Soviet embassy in Washington to send him and his wife "any periodicals or bulletins which you may put out for the benefit of your citizens **living, for a time, in the U.S.A.**" Later he also told New Orleans police officer Francis E. Martello that he was in America **"only temporarily"** and planned to return to Russia, as documented in the Warren Commission Report.

DEVELOPING THE SECRET INK

HERE IS THE TRANSLATION OF MARINA'S LETTER, WITH A TRANSCRIPTION OF OSWALD'S ATTACHED NOTE.

Dear Comrade Reznichenko!

I received two letters from you in which you requested me to indicate the reason for my wish to return to the USSR.

But first of all, permit me to apologize for such a long silence on my part and to thank you for the considerate attitude toward me on the part of the Embassy. The reasons for my silence were certain family "problems" (so to speak), which stood in the way. That is also one of the reasons why I wish to return to the Homeland. The main reason is "of course" homesickness, regarding which much is written and spoken, but one learns it only in a foreign land.

I count among family "problems" the fact that at the middle or end of October I expect the birth of a 2nd child. This would probably complicate matters for me, because I would not be able to work for the first few months. But there is no one I could expect to help me, for I have no parents. My relatives were against my going to America and therefore I would be ashamed to appeal to them. That is why I had to weigh everything once more before replying to your letter.

But things are improving due to the fact that my husband expresses a sincere wish to return together with me to the USSR. I earnestly beg you to help him in this. There is not much that is encouraging for us here and nothing to hold us. I cannot work for the time being, even if I did find a job. And my husband is often unemployed. It is very difficult for us to live here. We do not have the money for me to come to the Embassy, not even to pay for the hospital, etc. in connection with the birth of the baby. We both beg you very very much to help make it possible for us to return to live and work in the USSR.

In my application I did not specify the place where I would like to live in the Soviet Union. I earnestly beg you to help us obtain permission to live in Leningrad, where I grew up and went to school. There I have a sister and brother from my mother's second marriage. I know that I do not have to explain to you the reason for my wanting to live precisely in that city. It speaks for itself. I permit myself to write this without any wish to belittle the merits of our other cities. Moreover, it is easier for me to find a job in Leningrad, since there are more pharmacies there and they need more employees. For instance, when I came from Leningrad to Minsk, I could not find work in my field for quite a long time, because there were plenty of employees there.

These are the main reasons why my husband and I wish to return to the USSR. Please do not deny our request. Make us happy again, help us get back what we lost through our foolishness. We hope our second child will also be born in the USSR.

Sincerely and respectfully,
M. Oswald

P.S. I enclose with this letter my husband's application requesting permission to enter the USSR.

July 1, 1963

Dear Sirs

Please rush the entrance visa for the return of Soviet citizen Marina N. Oswald. She is going to have a baby in October, therefore you must grant the entrance visa. I make the transportation arrangements before then. As for my return entrance visa please consider it separtably.

Thank you
Lee H. Oswald

DEVELOPING THE
SECRET INK

CONVENTIONAL WISDOM :   The KGB/PGU showed no interest in Oswald.

FACT :   In 1962 Oswald was sent back to the United States by the PGU, bringing with him a PGU-fabricated cover story about the years he had spent in the Soviet Union.

DOCUMENTARY EVIDENCE :   Oswald's "Historic Diary." This is a fascinating document that purports to detail Oswald's life in the Soviet Union, and it also signifies the "historical" importance of his mission in the U.S. In 1961 the PGU (and its Romanian counterpart, the DIE) introduced fabricated diaries to help their agents sent abroad remember what they had supposedly done. (Before 1961, such agents had usually taken their fabricated biographical data with them on soft film hidden inside some personal object, such as a hairbrush; however, if found, that constituted a corpus delicti.) The new procedure was usually for a PGU disinformation expert to prepare such a diary and for the agent to copy it out in his own handwriting.

"Historic Diary" page containing Briticisms.

A qualified American handwriting expert (Dr. Thea Stein Lewinson) has judged Oswald's **diary to have been written in two sittings**. It contains a few **British spellings and expressions** as well as awkward English phrases. Why? Because the PGU did not have any teachers of American English until 1964. Here are some examples of such Briticisms: Rosa is "very merry and kind;" the receptionist "points at a large lager and says…please register;" "Alferd is a Hungarian chap."

Oswald's "Historic Diary" must have also been drafted in a rush after Oswald applied to go back to the United States, judging by such **anachronisms** as giving a figure in new rubles for January 1960 when the ruble devaluation did not take place until a year later.

"Historic Diary" page containing anachronisms.

DEVELOPING THE SECRET INK

CONVENTIONAL WISDOM : Marina was born in Severodvinsk, a small town in Archangel Oblast, a remote area of the Soviet Union prohibited to Westerners, according to the birth certificate she brought with her from the Soviet Union.

FACT : Marina was surely *born in Leningrad.* Her birth certificate, issued on July 19, 1961—although Marina would have needed one for her wedding on April 30, 1961—was certainly faked.

DOCUMENTARY EVIDENCE : On May 5, 1961, Oswald wrote his brother Robert: "On April 30 of this year I got married. My wife ... was born in the city of Leningrad." In another letter, postmarked May 16, 1961, in Moscow, Oswald informed the United States embassy there that he had gotten married, saying: "My wife is Russian, born in Leningrad, she has no parents living and is quite willing to

Oswald's 1961 letter to the U.S. embassy in Moscow stating Marina was born in Leningrad.

DEVELOPING THE
SECRET INK

leave the Soviet Union with me and live in the United States." George Bouhe, a Russian émigré living in Texas who met the Oswalds there, is on record as having admired Marina's pure Leningrad accent. Evidently, the PGU changed the record of Marina's birthplace—and very likely her name—to an area where her family circumstances could not be checked by U.S. officials.

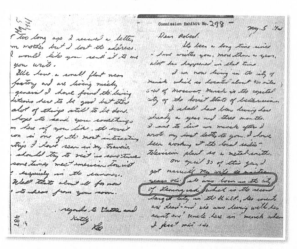

Oswald's letter to his brother stating Marina was born in Leningrad.

DEVELOPING THE
SECRET INK

CONVENTIONAL WISDOM : Oswald's best American "friend," the "aristocratic" baron George de Mohrenschildt, was not linked in any way with the assassination of President Kennedy. In *Case Closed,* Gerald Posner states: "The KGB informed this author in 1992 that it had no file on de Mohrenschildt or his wife, Jeanne, indicating neither had worked for it." (p. 86)

FACT : George de Mohrenschildt was a Soviet illegal officer endowed with three consecutive biographies to accommodate his intelligence tasks. Before WWII he was documented by Moscow as Baron von Mohrenschildt, son of a German director of the Swedish "Nobel interests," and was used to infiltrate Nazi organizations. After WWII he became the French George de Mohrenschildt, who had attended a school in Belgium founded by Napoleon, and he was directed to penetrate the CIA. During the Cold War, Moscow transformed his father into a Russian engineer in the Ploiesti oilfields in Romania, captured there by the Soviet Army and executed. De Mohrenschildt was Oswald's support officer in the U.S. In 1977, de Mohrenschildt killed himself just hours after getting a subpoena to retestify to the House Select Committee on Assassinations.

Oswald's picture with inscriptions dedicated to de Mohrenschildt.

DOCUMENTARY EVIDENCE : Picture of Oswald holding his rifle, inscribed: "To my friend George from Lee, 5/IV/63." This picture was presented to the House Select Committee on Assassinations by de Mohrenschildt's widow three days after he committed suicide, together with a 245-page manuscript entitled *I am a Patsy!* On the back of the

DEVELOPING THE SECRET INK

picture, Marina wrote in Russian: "hunter of fascists! Ha! Ha! Ha!" In the manuscript de Mohrenschildt claimed he knew nothing about this picture, allegedly discovered by his wife in a storage box in 1967, and he speculated that Oswald had in a sense left "a gift for us from beyond his grave."

In reality, the de Mohrenschildts did meet the Oswalds on April 5, 1963. Ten days later Oswald took a shot at Gen. Walker and immediately went to Mexico City to brag to the PGU that he had escaped without detection. On April 19, the de Mohrenschildts precipitously moved to Haiti, without even saying goodbye to the Oswalds.

255

to see if the records were not broken, she shrieked almost hysterically

"Look, there is a picture of Lee Oswald here!"

This was the same, so controversial picture of Lee, which appeared on the cover the the defunct "Life". Many newspapermen and "investigators" had assumed and had written hundreds of pages that this picture was a fabrication, a "fake", a superimposed photograph. Frankly we did not care but now, right there, was a proof that the picture was genuine

We stood literally frozen stiff, Lee staring at us in his martial pose, the famous rifle in his hands, like in a Marine parade. It was a gift for us from beyond his grave.

"What did he mean by leaving this picture to us?" I wondered aloud. "He was not a vain kind of a person."

Then Jeanne shouted excitedly again:"look there is an inscription here. It read:"To my dear friend George from Lee." and the date follow - April 1963, at the time when we were thousand of miles away in Haiti I kept looking at the picture and the inscription deeply moved, my thoughts going back when Lee was alive.

Then I slowly turned the picture photograph and there was another

256

epitaph, seemingly in Marina's handwriting, in Russian. In translation it reads;" this is the hunter of fascists! Ha! HA! Ha!"

Here Marina was making fun of her husband, jeering Lee's very serious anti-fascist feelings, which we knew so well and described in several chapters of this book.

It's hard to describe the impact of this discovery on us, especially Lee's dedication and Marina's inscription. This message from beyond the grave was amazing and shocking. From the grave we did not even dare to visit, because FBI considered with suspicion all the visitors at Lee's burial place. The confirmation that Lee considered me his best friend flattered me but Marina's message expressed a chilling scorn for her husband. Anyway, if he were a hunter of fascists, and we agree with such a description, why was she making fun of him?

First of all it makes in doubt her assertion that Lee tried to shoot General Walker, secondly for a Soviet Russian refugee the word "fascist" is not a laughing matter - some fifteen million people lost their lives fighting them. And how many more died of cold and hunger?

We kept this photograph for ourselves and showed it only to a few close friends. Their reactions were interesting: to some the photograph indicated that Lee was a maniac, a killer, it constituted a proof of

De Mohrenschildt manuscript's pages 255 and 256.

DEVELOPING THE
SECRET INK

CONVENTIONAL WISDOM :　　Today most Americans believe that Kennedy's assassination was the result of some home-based conspiracy involving the CIA, other elements of the U.S. government, or organized crime.

FACT :　　The conspiracy theories originated with the KGB, then gradually took off on their own. The intelligence services of the entire Soviet bloc were tasked to divert public attention on the assassination away from Moscow and toward elements of the U.S. itself. The Romanian part of that operation, codenamed Dragon, was so secret that Pacepa had to write out its plan by hand, in one single copy.

DOCUMENTARY EVIDENCE :　　The first assassination book published in the United States, *Oswald: Assassin or Fall Guy?*, had as author Joachim Joesten, a German-born American Communist identified as a PGU agent in the

Oswald:

Assassin
Or
Fall Guy?

Joachim
Joesten

Marzani & Munsell Publishers Inc.

Title page of Joesten/PGU book.

DEVELOPING THE
SECRET INK

Mitrokhin Archive (25,000 pages of PGU documents smuggled from Moscow by British intelligence). The book was published by another Mitrokhin-identified Soviet agent, Carlo Aldo Marzani (PGU codename Nord), who owned Liberty Book Club (PGU codename Sever) in New York. According to documents in the Mitrokhin Archive, Marzani received $80,000 from the PGU to produce pro-Soviet books, plus an annual $10,000 to advertise them aggressively. Joesten's book was enthusiastically reviewed by a Venona-identified PGU agent, Victor Perlo, and was vigorously promoted by a PGU-published magazine, *New Times* (*Novoye Vremya*). Joesten's book alleges that Oswald was "an FBI agent provocateur with a CIA background" who became a "perfect fall guy" in the assassination devised by "some officials of the CIA and FBI" and by "reactionary oil billionaires such as H. L. Hunt."

Joesten dedicated his book to Mark Lane, an American undercover Communist writer, who in 1966 produced the bestseller *Rush to Judgment*, alleging that Kennedy was assassinated by a right-wing American group. In 1967 Joesten "authored" *The Case Against Lyndon Johnson in the Assassination of President Kennedy* and *Oswald: The Truth*, soon followed by *A Citizen's Dissent* (1968) by Mark Lane. The latter also helped New Orleans district attorney Jim Garrison arrest a local man, whom he accused of conspiring with elements of U.S. intelligence to murder Kennedy in order to stop his efforts to end the Cold War. Garrison's *On the Trail of the Assassins* was one of the books that inspired Oliver Stone's movie *JFK*.

The Kennedy conspiracy era was born.

To Mark Lane

The brilliant and courageous New York attorney whose "Brief For Oswald," published in *National Guardian* newsweekly, December 19, 1963, was the opening shot in a campaign that will not end until the Myth of the Demented Assassin has been thoroughly destroyed, and the real killer of John F. Kennedy is brought to book. Like Emile Zola's *J'Accuse*, Mark Lane's "Brief For Oswald" will go down in history as one of the great libertarian documents, a monument to free men's determination to seek and tell the truth against all odds. Neither the "police state" tactics of the FBI—to use his own words—nor the conspiracy of silence of the press magnates, could sway him from doggedly pursuing the truth. The Private Citizens Committee of Inquiry, which he founded and heads, may not have received one-millionth of the press attention that has gone to the Warren Commission, yet it is the only citizens' organization which has independently developed a body of evidence and will continue to do so until the truth is fully established. I also wish to express in this context my sincere admiration and sympathy for Mrs. Marguerite Oswald, who has borne the ignominies heaped upon her by the news fabricators with composure, while fighting to clear her son's name.

Joesten's dedication of his book to Mark Lane.

DEVELOPING THE SECRET INK

CONVENTIONAL WISDOM : American graphological experts certified that a letter addressed to "Mr. Hunt," dated November 8, 1963, and signed Lee Harvey Oswald, copies of which turned up in the United States in 1975, was written by Oswald. Conspiracy theorists connected the letter to the CIA's E. Howard Hunt, by then well known from the Watergate affair, and used it to "prove" that the CIA was implicated in the Kennedy assassination.

FACT : Oswald's Hunt letter was forged by the PGU twelve years after Oswald died. The above-mentioned PGU book *Oswald: Assassin or Fall Guy?* blames, among others, right-wing Texas oil barons such as H. L. Hunt for the assassination. When former CIA officer E. Howard Hunt began making news in the Watergate scandal, the PGU took advantage of the name similarity and disseminated the ambiguous "Dear Mr. Hunt" letter.

DOCUMENTARY EVIDENCE : The Mitrokhin Archive contains PGU documents certifying that the "Hunt Letter" was forged by the PGU during the Watergate scandal. The forged PGU letter was twice checked for "authenticity" by the KGB's Technical Operations Directorate (OTU) and approved for use. In 1975, the PGU mailed three photocopies from Mexico to conspiracy buffs in the United States. (The PGU rules allowed only photocopies of counterfeited documents to be used, to avoid close examination of the original).

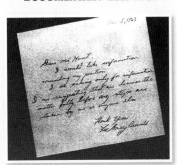

The "Dear Mr. Hunt" letter falsified by the PGU.

DEVELOPING THE SECRET INK

CONVENTIONAL WISDOM : A 245-page manuscript by George de Mohrenschildt entitled *I am a Patsy!*—described as the last words spoken by Oswald—which came to light immediately after de Mohrenschildt's suicide, is regarded as a genuine document that sheds light on how he perceived Oswald and his role in the assassination.

FACT : George de Mohrenschildt's manuscript contradicts numerous statements he made under oath, without any apparent reason.

DOCUMENTARY EVIDENCE : The similarity between de Mohrenschildt's diary and that of the PGU book *Oswald: Assassin or Fall Guy?* suggests that both may have been conceived at the Lubyanka. Both the book and the manuscript assert that Oswald was of no use to Soviet intelligence, both go to great lengths to generate sympathy for him, both present Oswald as an admirer of President Kennedy, and both discredit the idea that Oswald committed the crime. Both also extol the Soviet Union. Here is the ode to Khrushchev sung by de Mohrenschildt, a self-proclaimed American aristocrat who allegedly dedicated his life to fighting Communism: *"He is gone now. God bless his Bible-quoting soul and his earthy personality. His sudden bursts of anger and beating on the table with his shoe, are all gone and belong to history. Millions of Russians miss him."*

204

Lee himself mentioned it, caressing the child:"look, she is much better-looking now than our great Russian leader."

"I hope she keeps his amusing and friendly personality," said Jeanne.

He is gone now, God bless his Bible-quoting soul and his earthy personality. His sudden bursts of anger and beating of the table with his shoe, are all gone and belong to history. Millions of Russians miss him.

After this Easter visit things began to move so fast for us that we could not see the Oswalds and we did not even talk to them on the phone.

De Mohrenschildt's manuscript, page 204.

CHAPTER 6

THE KILLING OF PRESIDENT KENNEDY

A s a youth, paradoxically, Stalin attended a theological seminary—from which, however, he was expelled. Mass murder would only come later. Khrushchev rose to ultimate power because he too was willing to kill. Strongly supportive of Stalin's Great Purge of the 1930s, Soviet documents show that during the years in which he was leader of the Ukraine, Khrushchev was responsible for killing over 30,000 people.[1] From his memoirs we know that a few days after Stalin died, Khrushchev conducted a palace coup during the June 26, 1953, meeting of the Soviet Presidium aimed at killing off the powerful head of the Soviet Union's political police, Lavrentiy Beria, who was now his rival for the vacant Soviet throne. As related in his own account, Khrushchev came to the meeting with a gun in his pocket and played the main role from beginning to end.

"I prodded [Premier Georgy] Malenkov with my foot and whispered: 'Open the session and give me the floor.' Malenkov went white; I saw he was incapable of opening his mouth. So I jumped up and said: 'There is one item on the agenda: the anti-Party, divisive activity of imperialist agent Beria.'"[2]

According to Khrushchev, after proposing that Beria be relieved of all his party and government positions, "Malenkov was still in a state of panic. As I recall, he didn't even put my motion to a vote. He pressed a secret button, which gave the signal to the generals who were waiting in

79

the next room."³ With Beria under arrest, Khrushchev easily wrested the top job away from his closest ally, Malenkov.

On December 24, 1953, the Soviet media announced that Minister of Interior Lavrentiy Beria, together with former chief of the secret political police Vsevolod Merkulov, chief of foreign intelligence Vladimir Dekanozov, and five other top members of the Soviet political police had all been found guilty of working for Western intelligence and had been executed.⁴ Khrushchev then appointed General Aleksandr Sakharovsky, formerly the brutal chief Soviet advisor for Romania's political police, the Securitate, as head of this new PGU.

After crushing the Hungarian revolution and hanging Imre Nagy and its other leaders in 1956, Khrushchev promoted political murder as his primary foreign policy tool. Gen. Pacepa and the other leaders of the Soviet bloc intelligence community were told that Stalin had made one inexcusable mistake—he had aimed the cutting edge of his security apparatus against the Soviet Union's own people. In his famous "secret" speech criticizing Stalin, Khrushchev said he intended to correct that error. Therefore he ordered his espionage service to form components in all "sister" services in the Soviet bloc to carry out secret assassinations in the West. Soviet satellites were useful at giving cover to Soviet-ordered operations. The Romanian assassination component was called "X," the last letter of the alphabet. It was managed by DIE General Tanasescu, former chief of the DIE station in Austria.

Our real enemies were in the West, not in the Soviet bloc, Moscow informed the management of the Romanian espionage service of those days. One of the first killing operations conducted under the new rules was the secret kidnapping and execution of anti-Communist émigré leader Oliviu Beldeanu out of West Germany. This was carried out in September 1958 jointly among the KGB, the East German Stasi, and the Romanian espionage service. Official East German and Romanian newspapers blamed the CIA, repeating official communiqués stating that Beldeanu had been arrested in East Germany following a secret CIA infiltration to carry out sabotage and diversion operations. In reality, Beldeanu was kidnapped from West Berlin.

Then came the public trial of Bogdan Stashinsky in October 1962 by the West German Supreme Court. A KGB officer stationed in East Berlin, Stashinsky had defected to West Germany. He confessed to having assassinated two leading Ukrainian émigrés in 1957 and 1959 in West Germany on Khrushchev's orders. Khrushchev had decorated him for these crimes with the highest Soviet medal, he said. It was, at least in Europe, a PR debacle for Khrushchev as the brutal criminality of his policy of international assassination was officially exposed to the world.

The Stashinsky trial received substantial publicity in the West, including a discussion in a previous book by Pacepa dealing with the KGB's worldwide disinformation operation, codenamed Dragon, about how it sought to conceal its hand in President Kennedy's assassination.[5] The Stashinsky trial turned into a trial of Khrushchev, refuting Khrushchev's carefully constructed effort to depict the Soviet Union and its KGB as having sharply departed from Stalin's practices. The Stashinsky trial showed that this image was definitively untrue. Khrushchev had merely turned assassinations abroad. He had personally ordered the killings committed by Stashinsky and had personally decorated him with the Order of Lenin, the highest Soviet medal.[6]

In January 1961 Gen. Sakharovsky informed the management of the DIE that President Kennedy had become a puppet in the hands of the CIA. A few months later, Kennedy humiliated Khrushchev into abandoning his efforts to gain control of all of Berlin, which meant that instead of walling off the Soviet sector, Pacepa's DIE was now tasked to "throw mud on the Pig"—the PGU's new code name for Kennedy.

On October 26, 1959, a few weeks after visiting the United States, Khrushchev landed in Bucharest for what would become known as his six-day vacation in Romania, his longest vacation abroad. However, his stay in Romania was not really a vacation. Khrushchev's secret goal during his trip to Washington was to snatch West Berlin from Eisenhower's hands. At that time Pacepa was chief of Romania's intelligence station in West Germany and was minutely informed about the conversations with the Soviet leader. After the death of Secretary of State John Foster Dulles, President Dwight Eisenhower had assumed a more personal role in the conduct of American foreign policy.

"We'll get [West] Berlin," Khrushchev assured Romanian leader Gheorghe Gheorghiu-Dej. Khrushchev had inherited his obsession with Germany from Stalin. Germany was the cradle of Marxism, Karl Marx's birthplace, and it was a matter of personal pride for Khrushchev to see that it be communist. Khrushchev did not get West Berlin. On August

13, 1961, he was forced to erect the infamous Berlin Wall and to proclaim it a great victory.

In October 1962, the United States learned from Oleg Penkovsky, a heroic Soviet military intelligence officer who had volunteered his information to the United States, that in payback for his failure to get West Berlin, Khrushchev was trying to turn Cuba into a Soviet nuclear base from which to attack the U.S. Gheorghiu-Dej happened to be in Moscow during the critical days of the Cuban crisis following a state visit to Indonesia and Burma. Dej stopped off in Moscow for a couple of hours to inform Khrushchev about the results of his visits. And there he stayed.

Just before Dej's trip, President Kennedy had publicly warned Moscow to refrain from any dangerous adventure in Cuba. Khrushchev, who at critical moments always reached out for an audience, needed to vent his anger on somebody. Without even asking Dej what his program for the day was, Khrushchev commanded that a state luncheon and festive evening at the opera be held in Dej's honor, both to be attended by the whole Soviet Presidium and widely publicized by the Soviet media as a display of communist unity. During that state luncheon, Khrushchev swore at Washington, threatened to "nuke" the White House, and cursed loudly every time anyone spoke the words "America" or "American."

The next morning, Dej was having breakfast with Khrushchev when KGB chairman General Vladimir Yefimovich Semichastny handed Khrushchev a KGB cable from Washington. It stated that Kennedy had ordered a naval "quarantine" to prevent the eighteen Soviet cargo ships heading toward Cuba from reaching their destination. According to Dej's account, when Khrushchev finished reading the cable, he "cursed like a bargeman," threw it on the floor, and ground his heel into it. "That's how I'm going to crush that viper," he spat, meaning Kennedy. Back in Bucharest, Dej, in describing Khrushchev's rage, said, "If Kennedy had been there, the lunatic would have strangled him dead on the spot."

On October 28, 1962, Khrushchev backed down in the face of fierce American resistance and ordered his ships loaded with nuclear rockets to turn away from the confrontation. It happened to be Pacepa's birthday, and Dej celebrated both events with champagne. "That's the end of the lunatic," Dej predicted. He hated Khrushchev.

The following year, John F. Kennedy's assassination on November 20, 1963, sent the United States into shock. An age of peace and innocence had abruptly come to an end. Then Lee Harvey Oswald, Kennedy's accused assassin, was himself killed by Jack Ruby two days later, live in front of national television cameras. The Dallas police and the FBI quickly identified Oswald as the lone assassin of the president. But the whole truth about this odious crime of the century is still in the dark.

The JFK assassination was one of the few episodes in the Cold War where both sides had an interest in hiding the truth. After the humiliations of his erection of the Berlin Wall in 1961 and the withdrawal of his nuclear missiles from Cuba in 1962, Khrushchev lost the confidence of the Soviet Union's governing elite. The October 1962 trial of Stashinsky at the West German Supreme Court depicted Khrushchev to the West as just another odious butcher. It was not true that after the XXth Party Congress, Khrushchev had stopped the KGB's killings—he had merely turned its focus abroad.

Lyndon Johnson's and Khrushchev's interests happened to coincide on the JFK assassination. The assassination of Archduke Franz Ferdinand by Serbian terrorist Gavrilo Princip in 1914 had set off the First World War; President Johnson reasonably feared JFK's assassination might ignite the first nuclear war. Therefore, on November 29, he created a blue-ribbon commission, the Warren Commission, named after its chairman, Chief Justice Earl Warren, invoking the integrity of its distinguished members to hush even the slightest rumor of "foreign complications" stemming from Oswald's known defection to the Soviet Union and his connections with Cuba. Gen. Pacepa has described the KGB's operation to hide its hand in the JFK assassination, codenamed on the Romanian end "Dragon," in an earlier book.[7] Thus, the interest of both the U.S. and the USSR in hiding the truth allowed a KGB disinformation operation, also aimed at diverting attention away from the KGB's connection with Oswald, to achieve currency.[8]

The Warren Commission did not actually begin its field investigation on the JFK assassination until March 18, 1964, after the trial of Jack Ruby, Oswald's assassin, had ended.

On June 15, 1964, when everyone had already learned from KGB disinformation that the Soviet Union had not been involved in JFK's assassination, the Warren Commission finally announced that it had completed the investigation. Its final report was *not* written by intelligence experts but by three lawyers (Norman Redlich, Alfred Goldberg, and Lee Rankin) who had no experience in foreign counterintelligence and had never heard of KGB patterns and codes. It was like charging carpenters to perform heart surgery. The lawyers also worked under constant pressure from the commission to close doors rather than open them because of the time pressure to complete the report before the upcoming presidential election.

The Warren Commission report, published by the Government Printing Office on September 24, 1964, did not address the multitude of KGB-sponsored books already published in the West that accused the U.S. of killing President Kennedy, although these books had already become popular items. The Commission report consists of twenty-six volumes of testimonies to the commission, documents obtained primarily from federal and state authorities and from the Soviet government, plus one volume containing the summary report. The summary report, which can be found in most public libraries, is a disorganized hodgepodge of material assembled by various staff members, to which is attached an unsatisfactory index. Nevertheless, the complete publication contains a wealth of raw information that, to an informed analyst with Soviet intelligence experience, shows the Soviet hand.

SOVIET FINGERPRINTS

The FBI once told the U.S. Congress that only a native Arabic speaker could catch the fine points of an al-Qaeda telephone intercept, especially one containing doublespeak and codes. Both coauthors of this book are familiar with both doublespeak and codes. In the intelligence community, everything of even relative importance is expressed in doublespeak or in code. In the Soviet bloc intelligence community, even the names of the officers were in code. In 1955, when Pacepa became a foreign intelligence officer, he was told that his name there would be Mihai Podeanu, and Podeanu he remained until 1978 when he broke with communism. All his subordinates used codes in their written reports and even in conversations with their own colleagues. When Pacepa left Romania for good, his espionage service was the "university," the country's leader was the "architect," Vienna was "Videle," and so on.

Espionage operations can be easily isolated out by their particular codes if you are familiar with them. Counterintelligence experts call them "operational evidence" and accord them the same credibility as police investigators give to DNA and fingerprint evidence.

The twenty-six volumes of the Warren Commission Report contain dozens of KGB codes and operational patterns. But to the best of our knowledge, none were identified by the Warren Commission because of its members' lack of familiarity with KGB codes and patterns. Here is one example of codes published by the Warren Commission but ignored by its analysts and the writers of its final report, who were lawyers, not intelligence officers.

On April 10, 1963, a shot was fired at American General Edwin Walker at his home in Dallas, Texas. The incident was reported in the local American news, and the bullet was recovered, but no evidence turned up at the time that could help identify the perpetrator.

After Oswald's arrest for the assassination of President Kennedy, the bullet taken from Walker's house was examined by ballistics experts, who concluded that it could have been fired by Oswald's Mannlicher-Carcano rifle.[9]

On December 2, 1963, ten days after Kennedy's assassination, the Dallas police found, at the house where Oswald's wife, Marina, was staying, an undated note in Oswald's handwriting, which must have been written just before he took the shot at Walker on April 10, 1963. The note consists of instructions in Russian to his wife on what to do if he should be arrested or worse. Here is its English translation (emphasis as in the original):

1. This is the KEY to the mailbox of the main post office, found in the city, on ERVAY street the same street where the drugstore is where you always stood. 4 blocks from the drugstore on the same street to the post office there you will find our box. I paid for the box last month so don't worry about it.

2. Send the embassy the information about what happened to me and also clip from the newspaper, (if anything is written about me in the paper) I think the embassy will quickly help you when it knows everything.

3. I paid for the house on the 2nd so don't worry about that.

4. I also paid for the water and gas not long ago.

5. It is possible there will be money from work, they will send to our box at the post office. Go to the bank and change the check into cash.

6. My clothes etc. you can throw out or give away. Do not keep them. But my PERSONAL papers (military, factory, etc.) I prefer that you keep.

7. A few of my documents are in the blue small valise.

8. The address book is on my table in the study, if you need it.

9. We have friends here and the Red Cross will also help you. (Red Cross [sic] in English.)

10. I left you money as much as I could, 60$ on the 2nd, and you and June can live on 10$ a week 2 months more.

11. If I am alive and they have taken me prisoner, the city jail is located at the end of that bridge that we always rode over when we went into town (the very beginning of the city after the bridge). [10]

As it turned out, Oswald succeeded in firing a shot at General Walker and getting away without attracting any attention to himself, just as he must have hoped. Marina would tell the Warren Commission that "[w]hen he fired, he did not know whether he had hit Walker or not," and that when he learned from the newspaper the next day that he had missed only because Walker moved his head, Oswald "was very sorry that he had not hit him."[11] The fact that he fired only once[12] supports the theory that this was primarily a test exercise for Oswald to prove that he would be able to escape clean from a real assassination in the U.S.

It is also significant that on July 1, 1963, Oswald sent a letter to the Soviet embassy in Washington asking to "Please rush the entrance visa for the return of Soviet citizen Marina N. Oswald. She is going to have a baby in October, therefore you must grant the entrance visa. I make the transportation arrangements before then. As for my return entrance visa please consider it separatbly [sic]."

The Warren Commission, however, stated with a straight face that there was no connection, whatsoever, between the Soviet Union and the assassination of President Kennedy.

In the late 1970s, the U.S. House of Representatives, unhappy with the conclusions of the Warren Commission, formed the Select Committee on Assassinations and conducted its own investigations. In 1979 the House published twelve volumes of documents and hearings and one summary volume on the JFK assassination. This report does contain some important new, relevant factual material in the form of documents that had come to light after 1964 and interviews conducted by the committee that pointed more suggestively toward Moscow than the Warren Commission's materials. But because of its lack of Soviet intelligence experience, the House, too, was unable to properly evaluate what it had uncovered.

In its final report, the committee excluded a Soviet hand in the assassination by simply stating: "In fact the reaction of the Soviet Government as well as the Soviet people seemed to be one of genuine shock and sincere grief. The committee believed, therefore, on the basis of the evidence available to it, that the Soviet Government was not involved in the assassination."

Apparently the House committee, like the Warren Commission, did not remember that the Soviet government had always relied on deception—to the point of even falsifying the Moscow street maps and telephone books. Nor did anyone seem to remember that Khrushchev had boldly lied to President Kennedy in denying that the Soviets were putting missiles in Cuba.

THE KGB PATTERN

In essence, espionage is an accumulation of one-time operations (one-time recruitments, one-time agent meetings, one-time thefts, etc.) written in codes and carried out based on certain tried-and-true patterns rooted in the traditions of each espionage organization. In other words, espionage is a repetitive process like serial killing or serial bank robbery that follows predictable patterns generated by the idiosyncrasies of the perpetrator.

Here is an example of the KGB modus operandi in killing President Kennedy: According to the sworn testimony of Oswald's wife, Marina, after shooting at General Walker, Oswald put together a package, complete with photographs, showing how he had successfully planned the Walker operation. Afterward he traveled to Mexico City under a false identity (O. H. Lee) to show Soviet diplomat Valery Kostikov, whom Oswald called "Comrade Kostin," what he could do without being caught.

The CIA has publicly identified Valery Kostikov, aka "comrade Kostin," as an officer of the KGB's Thirteenth Department for assassinations abroad, known in the Soviet bloc's intelligence jargon as the Department for Wet Affairs (wet being a euphemism for bloody). According to the CIA, Kostikov had been assigned under diplomatic cover at the Soviet embassy in Mexico a short time before Oswald returned to the United States.

During the long holiday weekend of November 9–11, 1963, Oswald wrote a letter to the Soviet embassy in Washington in which he described the meeting he had just had in Mexico City with "comrade Kostin," whom he also named elsewhere as "Comrade Kostikov." After the assassination, a handwritten draft of that letter was found among Oswald's effects in the garage of Ruth Paine, an American at whose house Oswald had spent that weekend.

Ruth testified under oath that Oswald rewrote that letter several times before typing it on her typewriter. It was important to him. A photocopy of the final letter Oswald sent to the Soviet embassy was recovered by the Warren Commission. Let us quote from that letter, in which we have also inserted Oswald's earlier draft version in brackets:

"This is to inform you of recent events since my meetings with comrade Kostin [in draft: "of new events since my interviews with comrade Kostine"] in the Embassy of the Soviet Union, Mexico City, Mexico. I was unable to remain in Mexico [crossed out in draft: "because I considered useless"] indefinily because of my mexican visa restrictions which was for 15 days only. I could not take a chance on requesting a new visa [in draft: "applying for an extension"] unless I used my real name, so I returned to the United States."

The fact that Oswald used an operational codename for Kostikov confirms to us that both his meeting with Kostikov in Mexico City and his correspondence with the Soviet Embassy in Washington were conducted in a KGB operational context. The fact that Oswald did not use his real name to obtain his Mexican travel permit confirms this conclusion.

Now let us juxtapose this combined letter against the free guidebook *Esta Semana* (This Week) for September 28–October 4, 1963, and against a Spanish-English dictionary, both found among Oswald's effects. The guidebook has the Soviet embassy's telephone number underlined in pencil, the names Kosten and Osvald noted in Cyrillic on the page listing "Diplomats in Mexico," and checkmarks next to five movie theaters on the previous page.[13] In the back of his Spanish-English dictionary, Oswald wrote: "buy tickets [plural] for bull fight."[14] The Plaza México bullring is encircled on his Mexico City map.[15] Also marked on Oswald's map is the Palace of Fine Arts,[16] a favorite place for tourists to assemble on Sunday mornings to watch the Ballet Folklórico.

Contrary to what Oswald claimed, he was not observed at the Soviet embassy at any time during his stay in Mexico City, although the CIA had surveillance cameras trained on the entrance to the embassy at that time.[17]

All of the above facts taken together suggest to us that Oswald resorted to an unscheduled or "iron meeting"—*zheleznaya yavka* in Russian—for an urgent talk with KGB officer Valery Kostikov in Mexico City. The iron meeting was a standard KGB procedure for emergency situations, "iron" meaning ironclad or invariable.

In Pacepa's day his DIE approved quite a few iron meetings in Mexico City—a favorite place for contacting important agents living in the U.S.— and Oswald's iron meeting looks to us like a typical one. That means the following likely took place: a brief encounter at a movie house to arrange a meeting for the following day at the bullfights (in Mexico City they were held at 4:30 every Sunday afternoon), a brief encounter in front of the Palace of Fine Arts to pass Kostikov one of the bullfight tickets Oswald had bought, and a long meeting for discussions at the Sunday bullfight.

Of course, we cannot be sure that everything happened exactly that way. But in whatever way they connected, it is clear that Kostikov and Oswald did secretly meet over that weekend of September 28–29, 1963. The letter to the Soviet embassy that Oswald worked so hard on irrefutably proves that.

There is also plenty of proof that Oswald's Soviet wife, Marina, was also connected with the KGB. No assassination investigator has been able to decode this evidence because no one has ever built a KGB wife. General Pacepa did. In the mid-1980s, historian Michael Ledeen and Pacepa published a long article, ("La Grand Fauche") in the French magazine *L'Éxpress*, describing how Romania's foreign intelligence service, the DIE, had built a wife for a German adviser to NATO. The adviser threatened to sue the magazine, but *L'Éxpress* did not blink, and the NATO adviser disappeared from sight. The Library of Congress retranslated that *L'Éxpress* article into English and distributed it within the U.S. government.

Marina Nikolayevna Oswald looks like a carbon copy of "Andrea," the wife described in *L'Éxpress*. Here is one such similarity. In May 1961,

Oswald wrote to his brother Robert in the U.S. and to the U.S. embassy in Moscow telling them that he had gotten married and that his wife was born in the city of Leningrad. But the birth certificate Marina brought with her when she immigrated to the U.S. (issued on July 19, 1961, although she would have needed one for her marriage the previous April), shows that she was born in the remote northern town of Molotovsk (now Severodvinsk) in the northwest of the USSR.

Andrea's birthplace (Braşov, Romania) was also changed to a remote area where it would be unlikely for anyone in the West to be able to check. This practice was widely used by the KGB—and by General Pacepa's DIE.

Pacepa approved many other DIE biographies for "wives," and he can spot a few other holes in Marina's legend. In the U.S., for example, she claimed that her father had died before she was born and that she did not know anything about him, not even his name. She therefore allegedly took the name of her stepfather, Aleksandr Medvedev. In that case, her patronymic should have been Aleksandrovna, not Nikolayevna. Some of Gen. Pacepa's case officers also lost sight of such details.

Then there is her "uncle" in the KGB—a stock character who was en vogue at that time in the bloc foreign intelligence community. Those "uncles" were used to explain how the "wife" was able to rush the approval for her marriage and for her exit visa. "Andrea's" "uncle" was DIE Colonel Cristian Scornea, who had recruited her supposedly German husband. Marina had "Uncle Ilya," an NKVD colonel named Ilya Prusakov, who allegedly helped speed up the approval of her marriage to an American and to obtain her exit visa.

The "uncle in the KGB" continued for many years to play various roles in foreign and domestic KGB operations. Several Marines stationed at the U.S. embassy in Moscow in 1986 and carrying on affairs with local Soviet girls were eventually introduced to an "Uncle Sasha," who was actually a KGB officer who tried to recruit them. One of those Marines, Sgt. Clayton J. Lonetree (eventually sentenced for espionage), described how his relationship with Violetta Aleksandrovna Seina, a Soviet translator for English, grew from a chance meeting in a Moscow subway station into a series of clandestine rendezvous in a house ostensibly owned by her "Uncle Sasha." A few months later, Violetta introduced Lonetree to her "Uncle Sasha" himself at another meeting that also took place "in a subway station."[18] Another of those Marines, Corporal Arnold Bracy, was for his part accused by American authorities of failing to report personal contacts with an attractive Soviet cook and with her "Uncle Sasha."[19]

THE END OF KHRUSHCHEV

Russia can be unpredictable, but its past is prologue. During the years in which we coauthors still managed our countries' foreign intelligence communities, the world was flooded with official Russian news and intelligence information that Khrushchev had nothing to do with the assassination of President Kennedy.

In reality, Khrushchev himself was quietly arrested by the KGB a few months after the JFK assassination, and he never again became a free man.

On October 12, 1964, when Khrushchev and his close friend Anastas Mikoyan returned to Moscow from a long vacation in Pitsunda (Abkhazia), the KGB chairman, Vladimir Semichastny, was waiting for him at Vnukovo Airport. Semichastny informed Khrushchev that he was under arrest and asked him not to resist.

A few days later, the Politburo quietly accused Khrushchev of "harebrained schemes, hasty decisions, actions divorced from reality, braggadocio, and rule by fiat."[20] For the rest of his life, Khrushchev was kept under virtual house arrest.

When he died in 1971, the Soviet Politburo decreed that Khrushchev's erratic leadership had badly harmed the country. Therefore he was not worthy of burial inside the Kremlin Wall next to the other former leaders. The Soviet government even refused to pay for Khrushchev's gravestone. In 1972, Pacepa visited Khrushchev's grave in the Novodevichy Cemetery. There was only a small, insignificant marker identifying it.

CHAPTER 7

GHEORGHIU-DEJ, CEAUSESCU, AND "RADU"

S even days after Khrushchev was arrested by the KGB, Romania's communist ruler, Gheorghe Gheorghiu-Dej, concluded that the Kremlin was in a rout. He decided to take advantage of the confusion. On October 21, Dej called in the Soviet ambassador to Romania and asked him to withdraw the KGB advisors from Romania. Dej was tormented by the idea that the Kremlin was quietly using the KGB advisors in Romania to plan to kill him, just as the KGB had killed the communist leaders of Hungary and Czechoslovakia. It was in Dej's interest to have that potential source of danger closed off.

Moscow did not react well. The very next day, KGB chairman Vladimir Yefimovich Semichastny sent a scathing letter to his Romanian vassal, Minister of Interior Alexandru Draghici, pointing out that Romania was living under Moscow's "protective nuclear umbrella" and demanding that the KGB advisors be kept in place. A similar letter, couched in even harsher terms and signed by Soviet foreign intelligence chief Sakharovsky, landed on the desk of General Nicolae Doicaru, Romania's foreign intelligence chief at that time. In November, on just two hour's notice, General Sakharovsky arrived in Bucharest. Then General Semichastny himself put in an appearance. The discussions between Bucharest and Moscow regarding the withdrawal of the KGB advisors from Romania dragged on until the end of November 1964.

"We created the Securitate," was General Sakharovsky's refrain during

93

those November days. According to him, the Romanian request had set off a whole chain of explosions, from the KGB's Romanian desk all the way up to the KGB chairman. "Semichastny is raging mad," Sakharovsky emphasized. "He's ready to tear him limb from limb with his own two hands." "Him" meant Dej, who had good reason to believe Sakharovsky in this instance.

General Pacepa never met Semichastny, but on two separate occasions Sakharovsky told him that he was a wild and ambitious man who had recriminated harshly against Boris Pasternak and several other Soviet dissidents. "Iron Shurik" was also seeing red, Sakharovsky added, referring to Aleksandr Shelepin, the former KGB chairman, who by then was a Politburo member and secretary of the Central Committee with responsibility for the Red Army and the KGB.

In the end Dej got his way. In December 1964, the Romanian DIE became the first foreign intelligence service in the Warsaw Pact community to function without KGB advisers. To the best of our knowledge, it remained the only one until the 1989 revolutionary wave changed the face of Eastern Europe. Pacepa accompanied the KGB advisers in the DIE to the Bucharest North train station a couple of days before Christmas. There he ran into the Romanian minister of interior, Alexander Draghici, who was saying farewell to the KGB advisers in the domestic Securitate.

On Sunday, February 24, 1965, Pacepa paid his last visit to Gheorghiu-Dej, who had just come back from another trip to Moscow. As usual Pacepa found him with his best friend, Chivu Stoica. "This is for you," Dej said, handing Pacepa a leather-bound book by Karl Marx entitled *Notes on Romanians*. In his customary violet lead, Dej had inscribed the first page to Pacepa: "Well done!"

That was Dej's thanks to Pacepa for an intelligence operation that had paid off politically for Dej. In 1963 a DIE agent had come across four unfinished and never published manuscripts of Karl Marx's in the archives of the International Institute of Social History in Amsterdam that provided ammunition to contest the Soviet territorial claim to Romania's Bessarabia and Moldova. Dej ordered the manuscripts printed in the form of a booklet issued by the Romanian Academy but was reluctant to let it go on the open market, afraid it might blow too cold in Moscow's face.

Now, on that early spring day, Dej and Stoica decided to go for a walk in the garden. General Pacepa tagged along behind them. Dej complained of feeling weak, dizzy, and nauseous. "I think the KGB got me," he said, only half in jest.

"They got Togliatti," Stoica squeaked ominously. Palmiro Togliatti, the head of the Italian Communist Party, had died on August 21, 1964, while on a visit to the Soviet Union. There was a rumor going around at the top of the bloc's foreign intelligence community that he had been irradiated by the KGB on Khrushchev's order while vacationing in Yalta.

Togliatti's assassination was rumored to have been provoked by the fact that, while in the Soviet Union, he had written a "testament" in which he had expressed profound discontent with Khrushchev and suggested the need for fundamental changes in the Soviet Union's foreign policies. Togliatti reportedly questioned Khrushchev's honesty and criticized him for failing to understand the genesis of Stalinism using these words: "The most serious thing is a certain degree of scepticism with which some of those close to us greet reports of new economic and political successes. Beyond this must be considered in general as unresolved the origin of the cult of Stalin and how this became possible. To explain this solely through Stalin's serious personal defects is not completely accepted." Togliatti's frustrations were rumored to echo those of Leonid Brezhnev. In September 1964, *Pravda* published portions of Togliatti's testament. After that, Khrushchev was overthrown. This was seen as confirmation of those rumors.

Pacepa saw Dej shiver. He too had been critical of Khrushchev's foreign policy. Moreover, during the previous September he had expressed to Khrushchev his concern about Togliatti's "strange" death.

During the March 12, 1965, elections for Romania's Grand National Assembly, Gheorghiu-Dej went out to vote. A week later, he suddenly died of a brain hemorrhage. "Assassinated by Moscow" is what the new Romanian leader, Nicolae Ceausescu, whispered to Pacepa a few months after that. "Irradiated," he murmured in an even lower voice and added that it was "firmly established." The subject came up because Ceausescu had ordered Pacepa to secretly acquire the most sensitive Western radiation detection devices (based on Geiger-Müller counters) and install them throughout his offices and residences. In Ceausescu's view, Dej's "strange death" was proof that the KGB had improved its irradiation technique to reliable operational use.

Until he replaced Dej, Ceausescu had been a member of the Politburo in charge of managing Romania's security and armed forces. He was therefore thoroughly informed about KGB operations. When Pacepa discussed this subject with Ceausescu's personal physician, Dr. Abraham Schechter, Schechter agreed that Dej had been irradiated. "I have all the documents attesting to that," the physician said, adding that he was just waiting for a "favorable moment" to make them public.

Dr. Schechter was never able to disclose his documents, but in the spring of 1970 the Securitate received an irradiation weapon from Moscow that Moscow claimed would kill the target in less than a month—a new generation of the radioactive thallium used unsuccessfully in Germany against the Soviet defector Nikolay Khokhlov in 1954. "I told you they had it," Ceausescu remarked to Pacepa after he found out about the new weapon from the minister of interior. Ceausescu baptized it with the codename "Radu," from the Romanian *radiere* (radiation), and ordered the Securitate to try it out on some arrested dissidents who were on his enemies list. "It's not just free men who get sick and die," Ceausescu said with an evil wink. He also asked his personal physician—still Dr. Schechter—to study the new weapon and come up with supplementary measures to protect Ceausescu's offices, residences, and cars against a Soviet attempt to irradiate him.

In February 1973, the Securitate secretly purloined a letter and its attached medical documents from Dr. Schechter's apartment, attesting to Dej's irradiation as well as providing a technical description of the new KGB irradiation weapon, the "Radu." The minister of the interior, Ion Stanescu, informed Ceausescu that electronic coverage of Schechter showed that he was intending to smuggle the documents out to the West and publicize the KGB's use of lethal radiation against its targets. On March 15, 1973, Dr. Schechter just happened to "fall" out of a window and crash to the pavement below.

Ceausescu was sure the KGB had killed Dr. Schechter following a Securitate leak. A later investigation concluded that Dr. Schechter had indeed been murdered. "Masaryk revisited," Ceausescu remarked when he was informed about Dr. Schechter's death. Ceausescu was referring to Jan Masaryk, who had served as foreign minister in the Czechoslovakian government in exile during World War II and in the first postwar coalition government. In February 1948 Masaryk refused to resign his post as

Moscow demanded and, a few weeks later, "fell" out of a window at the Czechoslovakian Ministry of Foreign Affairs.

Ceausescu always stuttered when he was scared. "N-Now it's m-my t-turn!" Pacepa often came face-to-face with Ceausescu's paranoid fear of being killed by Moscow. Eventually he would wash his hands with alcohol after every handshake (even President Jimmy Carter's) and while abroad would eat only after a poison-tester had tried his food.

Less than an hour after learning of Dr. Schechter's death, Ceausescu fired Ion Stanescu, Romania's minister of interior and head of the Securitate, expelling him from the Political Executive Committee (the new name for the Politburo) of the Communist Party. Then Ceausescu called together the deputy ministers of interior in charge of managing the Securitate and the DIE and ordered that all Securitate officers who had graduated from the KGB school in Moscow be transferred into the reserves.

Once those steps had been taken, Ceausescu ran for cover. He put Romania's armed forces on alert, locked himself into his summer residence in Snagov some thirty miles north of Bucharest, and surrounded the whole area with tanks and armored vehicles belonging to the special military unit in charge of his personal security.

ASSASSINATIONS AS A FOREIGN POLICY TOOL

In June 1971, after returning from talks in China with Mao Zedong and Hua Guofeng (then minister of public security and, in 1977, China's supreme leader), Ceausescu told Pacepa and a couple of other close advisers that "the Kremlin has killed or tried to kill ten international leaders." "Ten," he repeated, counting them off on his fingers. First, Laszlo Rajk and Imre Nagy of Hungary. Lucretiu Patrascanu and Gheorghiu-Dej in Romania made four. Rudolf Slansky, the head of Czechoslovakia; Jan Masaryk, its chief diplomat; the shah of Iran (a book written by KGB defector Vladimir Kuzichkin a few years later minutely described this unsuccessful KGB operation[1]); Palmiro Togliatti of Italy; John F. Kennedy; and an attempt to kill Mao Zedong, which was botched.

After Gheorghiu-Dej's suspicious death, Ceausescu—now afraid for his own life—sought to align himself with Red China rather than the USSR. The Chinese were deeply concerned over a recent assassination attempt against Mao Zedong, planned with the help of Lin Biao, the head of the

Chinese Army, and organized by Moscow. Lin Biao had been educated in Moscow and still had a girlfriend there. When the plot failed, Lin Biao tried to escape to the Soviet Union but was killed when his plane crashed in Mongolia.

According to Mao and to Zhou Enlai, the KGB intended to use Chinese who had studied in Moscow to install a Soviet puppet government in Beijing. "All were Chinese security or military officers," Ceausescu explained, adding that Mao had now decided to purge the Chinese army and security police of all their Moscow-educated personnel.

"The B-Bear is a p-pig!" Ceausescu concluded, referring to Brezhnev. Ceausescu ordered DIE management to form a special counterintelligence unit to protect him from Soviet assassination. "You have one thousand personnel slots for this," Ceausescu told Pacepa. The new unit must be "nonexistent," he added—no name, no title, no sign on the door—invisibly concealed under the DIE umbrella, whose own existence was virtually unknown in Romania at that time. Ceausescu ordered that the unit be covered for operational purposes under U.M. 0920/A (in which U.M. meant "military unit," 0 signified a classified unit, 920 was the code number legally assigned to the DIE, and A indicated the brand-new unit).

The new undercover unit was housed in a large apartment building located within walking distance of Ceausescu's residence (on Rabat Street, next to the West German consulate). It was identified as the "Institute for Marketing."

To the best of our knowledge, U.M. 0920/A was the only major anti-KGB counterintelligence organization in the Soviet bloc. A couple of years later, U.M. 0920/A learned that Moscow was indeed after Ceausescu's scalp. That operation, codenamed "Dnestr," was activated in August 1969, a few days after a previously scheduled visit to Romania by Brezhnev and his prime minister, Aleksey Kosygin, had been cancelled and a year after Ceausescu publicly denounced the invasion of Czechoslovakia. Against Moscow's recommendation, Ceausescu had also invited President Richard Nixon to visit Romania a few days before the launch of "Dnestr."

As U.M. 0920/A would later learn, the Soviet Dnestr operation recruited seven Romanian military generals. All had been educated in the Soviet Union. Bucharest military garrison commander General Ion Serb and a few others were arrested by Ceausescu on trumped-up charges. The rest were shifted around from one job to another, making it difficult, if not impossible, for them to put down roots or for Moscow to maintain continuous, secret operational contact with them.

Just before Pacepa was granted political asylum in the United States in 1978, U.M. 0920/A uncovered another major KGB operation connected with the Dnestr plan. Lt. General Nicolae Militaru, a graduate of the Soviet Frunze Military Academy and now the commander of Romania's Second Military Region (Bucharest), had become a Soviet agent. Ceausescu was livid when told. He had just chosen Militaru for the position of first deputy minister of defense and chief of the General Staff.

In July 1978, when Pacepa reported to Ceausescu that Gen. Militaru had agreed to work for Moscow, the Romanian despot and his wife hid themselves inside their Snagov residence and had it surrounded by tanks. A Romanian proverb, however, says that what you fear is what you get.

THE END OF CEAUSESCU

On December 22, 1989, Romanian leader Nicolae Ceausescu was over-thrown by angry masses of people who had burst forth into the streets of Bucharest and other major cities of the country. Just hours after the popular uprising forced Ceausescu to flee in his helicopter, retired General Nicolae Militaru showed up at the Bucharest television station, now in the hands of the rebels, and appointed himself chief of Romania's armed forces. This was the same General Militaru who in 1978 had been picked up by microphones of the DIE's U.M. 0920/A at a secret meeting with a Soviet intelligence officer in Bucharest recruiting him for Moscow's Dnestr operation.[2]

Because Gen. Pacepa left Romania for good a few weeks after that report came in, he never learned if the Soviets had finalized General Militaru's recruitment. After Ceausescu's overthrow, however, Mihail Lupoi, a leader of the 1989 Romanian uprising who became minister of tourism in the first post-Ceausescu government but then had a falling out with it and defected to Switzerland, said in an interview published by the Italian newspaper *L'Unità* on March 1, 1990, that Militaru had become a Soviet intelligence agent. He indicated that evidence of Militaru's agent status could be found in a Securitate file codenamed "Corbu."

Shortly after Militaru appealed on television for other "comrade gen-erals" to unite against Ceausescu, Romania had a new surprise. Ion Ilich

Iliescu, a Moscow-educated member of Romania's Communist Party Politburo, whose father was so devoted to the founder of the Comintern that he named his son Ilich, stepped in front of Romanian television cameras and declared himself the chairman of an ad-hoc Provisional Committee for National Unity. U.M. 0920/A had begun monitoring Iliescu in 1972 because of his secret ties with Moscow.

The Western media quickly dug out an earlier report saying that Iliescu and Soviet leader Gorbachev had studied together in Moscow, where both had been party secretaries, one Soviet, the other for foreign students. The media also recalled a 1987 Iliescu article calling for "restructurare" (the Romanian word for perestroika, or restructuring), which he had published in the Romanian magazine *Romania Literara* and the West German magazine *Der Spiegel* had made known in the West.[3]

Originally, Iliescu was proud to acknowledge his acquaintance with Gorbachev. Dumitru Mazilu, a former intelligence colonel jailed as a dissident before Ceausescu's overthrow, who then became Iliescu's deputy in the Provisional Committee, told the Romanian media that Iliescu had called Gorbachev on the telephone during the Committee's first plenary session to report what he had already achieved.[4]

After that phone call, which Mazilu claimed to have personally witnessed, Iliescu suddenly denied that he had ever actually met Gorbachev. He admitted, however, that Ceausescu removed him from the Romanian Politburo after Gorbachev became the leader of the Soviet Union and that Ceausescu had kept him away from Bucharest when Gorbachev was visiting. Those facts about Iliescu's past were common knowledge in Romania by then. Moreover, in those early days of the revolution, Iliescu constantly emphasized that only Soviet-style glasnost and perestroika could save Romania.

What happened in Romania from that moment on no longer came as a surprise to us. Everything seemed inexorably to follow Moscow's Dnestr plan. The night of December 22, self-appointed President Ion Ilich Iliescu created the National Salvation Front as stipulated in the plan, which resembled KGB plans for the installation of puppet governments in Greece and Spain, and appointing himself as head. Another of U.M. 0920/A's prime targets due to his longstanding ties with Moscow was the ideologue of the 1989 Front, Silviu Brucan. Immediately after the Front came into being, Brucan acknowledged that it had Moscow's blessing. A couple of days later, however, he swallowed his own words when an "outraged" Eduard Shevardnadze, the Soviet foreign minister, vehemently denied there were any Soviet fingers in the events currently taking place in Romania.

At 2:00 p.m. on December 23, Romanian television announced that the National Salvation Front had asked the Soviet Union for military help, saying that "unidentified foreign terrorists" in Romania were trying to reinstate Ceausescu. That was exactly what the Dnestr plan had called for: to find a pretext for Soviet military intervention, which would occur should the coup not succeed on its own. The Soviet embassy promptly entered the picture, publicly stating that its personnel were in danger. In Moscow a few hours later, the Soviet television newscast Vremya stated that Ceausescu was being supported by "foreign mercenaries" (which was never proved). That night the Kremlin reportedly advised Iliescu that it would provide the military help he had requested. Misinformed and un-inspired, as it had been for years in Romanian affairs, the United States Department of State immediately announced that Washington would take a sympathetic view of Soviet military intervention in Romania.[5]

In the end the Kremlin was spared both the political and the financial cost of a military adventure in Romania. On that same December 23, the self-appointed president Iliescu announced that Ceausescu had been arrested the previous day, and a spokesman for the National Salvation Front promised that he would be given a public trial.[6] Nevertheless two days later, on Christmas Day, 1989, Romanian television came on the air with the news that the Ceausescu couple had been tried, sentenced to death, and executed by a military firing squad that same day. The loudly trumpeted videotape of the event was not broadcast until a day later.

Andrei Codrescu, an American writer and correspondent for National Public Radio, returned to visit his native Romania a few days after Ceausescu's killing. He conducted a thorough investigation of the events that followed. In a 1991 book, Codrescu concluded that the two Ceaus-escus' executioners, a professor of Marxism for Securitate officers at the Communist Party Academy (Virgil Magureanu) and an alleged astrologer previously sentenced as a common criminal by Ceausescu (Gelu Voicules-cu-Voican), were propelled to the top of Romania's leadership as soon as the dictator and his wife were dead, becoming respectively the head of Romania's new security police and the deputy prime minister.[7]

In 2019, former President Ion Ilich Iliescu, the chief of his political police Virgil Magureanu, and Romania's Deputy Prime Minister Gelu Voiculescu Voican were charged with crimes against humanity for their role in the aftermath of the violent revolt that toppled the communist regime in 1989.[8] According to Romania's prosecutor, 862 Romanians were killed in this event.

CHAPTER 8

THE GLASNOST SWINDLE

I n 1978, when Gen. Pacepa was granted political asylum by President Jimmy Carter, the Soviet Union's Communist Party was just a scramble of bureaucrats playing no greater role in the Soviet bloc than Lenin's embalmed corpse had in the Kremlin mausoleum.

According to our information, later confirmed by a well-documented post-Soviet biography, Russian president Mikhail Gorbachev was recruited by the KGB to spy on his classmates in the early 1950s while studying law at Moscow State University.[1] Gorbachev interned at the Lubyanka, the KGB headquarters,[2] where he came under the influence of Yuri Andropov, the first head of the KGB to sit on the Kremlin throne. Both had begun their careers in Stavropol. Andropov arranged for Gorbachev to be appointed to the Soviet Politburo. One Gorbachev biographer called him Andropov's "crown prince."[3]

Once in the Kremlin, Gorbachev and the KGB transformed glasnost into a political catchword carrying the new attribute of openness. Earlier, when Pacepa was at the top of the KGB community, glasnost was simply regarded as a disinformation tool. In the mid-1930s, the official Soviet encyclopedia defined the word "glasnost" as a spin on news released to the public: "Dostupnost obshchestvennomy obsuzhdeniyu, kontrolyu; publichnost," meaning, the quality of being made available for public discussion or control.[4][5]

Gorbachev did not intend to transform the Soviet Union into a liberal democracy. This is a point that he made clear in his books, speeches, and official pronouncements. Neither did any of his historical predecessors. Nor, in our opinion, has any Russian leader since the fall of the Berlin Wall. After all, even Peter the Great didn't cede any power to elected representatives when he replaced the Boyarskaya Duma with the Senate as the nation's supreme body, though the romantic notion that he had such a motive lives on.

The idea that Russia loves the West and wished to emulate its political institutions is a self-indulgent fancy peculiar to intellectuals in Western nations. Our view is that the truth is that, like Peter the Great before him, Gorbachev intended to save himself and his privileged circle in Russia's authoritarian structure from what they all knew to be communism's impending political and economic doom. In this he succeeded in the 1970s.

The clues that Gorbachev intended no real change after all, certainly none that might endanger his own absolute power, can be found in his discussion of communism as a system. The precariousness of the Soviet economy was caused by the personal greed of Leonid Brezhnev, his cronies and their families, and their antics, Gorbachev theorized. Corrupt individuals, not Marxism, had perverted the system, sullying a great nation. It was a crisis requiring his new leadership. It required major but not structural reform.

Stalin also used such reasoning in his public pronouncements at the very same time he was carrying out the most murderous purges in history. Remarkably, many believed the words while willfully ignoring the deeds. Mao, too, understood the use of the scapegoat. He periodically urged the Chinese to open up and criticize communism, a tactic that had the additional bonus of making it easier to later target anyone foolish enough to take him up on the invitation.

Gorbachev tactically applied criticism and the usual catchwords—bureaucratic inefficiency, corruption, nepotism, and alcohol—to convert the explosion of public contempt and resentment against a scapegoat and make it redound to political support for himself. At the same time, however, he insisted that communism's original, "positive" goals redeemed their abuse by some Russians.

Like Romania's Ceausescu, Gorbachev permitted local elections that were limited to two candidates, but he kept his own seat and those of his top *nomenklatura* off limits from the vote. Gorbachev's new "parliament" was just the old Supreme Soviet reshuffled to add a few hand-picked nonparty members and religious leaders. Russia's new "supreme governing body" was still the leader's docile servant. Gorbachev then installed himself into the newly renamed post of state president and gave himself broad governmental powers.

Russians followed along like sheep, as usual. Well-publicized meetings with the country's religious leaders were held so as to make it appear as if he favored an open society that would be soft on Christianity. The whole sequence of fake democratization had been trailblazed by Romania's Ceausescu. "Perfume your Communism with a dab of Western democracy, and the West will clothe you in gold," Andropov had told the Romanian leader. Ceausescu called it the Andropov Principle. Gorbachev's glasnost and perestroika were meant to instill hope and national pride as a necessary sop to the masses, to console them for getting little if any real democracy or food and consumer goods after the stirring reform moment had passed. Ceausescu's New Economic Order amounted to much the same thing.

It is important to note that the Kremlin was, and still is, a creature of habit. In Russia, any formulas for action that have proven successful in the past will always be repeated. For instance, Gorbachev's first visit to Washington in December 1987 was a near duplicate of Ceausescu's successful last official visit to the United States in April 1978. The latter visit had been prepared by Gen. Pacepa, who accompanied the Romanian tyrant on the actual visit.

Both leaders brought their foreign intelligence chiefs along with them. Both boosted their national history and culture and recited poems by famous writers. Both pretended to be fans of American movies. In Washington, both reaffirmed their deep devotion to Marxism and let everyone know that they were determined to stay in power for the rest of their lives—an anti-democratic fact, to be sure, but one that Washington nevertheless appreciated. Unfortunately, a foreign leader's determination to retain supreme power simplifies Washington's job, insofar as the conduct of foreign policy is concerned.

Both Gorbachev and Ceausescu also sought photo opportunities in the United States. They understood celebrity media manipulation well, and both went out of their way to make friends among the American media. Gorbachev arranged an exclusive NBC interview; Ceausescu's had been with the Hearst newspapers. After formal ceremonies, official document signing, and the requisite exchange of fancy dinners, Gorbachev again followed in Ceausescu's footsteps by turning on the charm for high-level American businessmen and members of Congress, too often all too eager to make themselves useful to visiting despots.

When Mikhail Gorbachev came to power in March 1985, he praised communism to the skies for domestic consumption. On February 25, 1986, he told the XXVIIth Congress of the Communist Party: "We have built the whole country anew, have made tremendous headway in the economic, cultural and social fields and have raised generations of builders of the new society. We have blazed the trail into outer space for humanity." Marshalling some alleged statistics: "In a quarter of a century, real per capita incomes have gone up 160 percent and the social consumption funds more than 400 percent; 54 million [apartments] have been built which enabled us to improve the living conditions of the majority of families.... The successes of our science, medicine and culture are universally recognized."[6] It was the classic Russian formula to boost national pride.

Gorbachev also set out to prove that he was a new breed of communist leader—just as Ceausescu had done. He called publicly for a decreased role for the party in running the country. It sounded terrific to Western ears. An evolution toward moderation! In fact, Gorbachev was seeking to outflank the competition. In the traditional exercise for any new Russian ruler, he was scapegoating the old regime. Everyone knew that the Communist Party was a dysfunctional and irrelevant bureaucracy. The secret police, not the party, had always been the source of political power in Russia—which is why nearly every Russian leader is so closely connected with the secret police.

In the spirit of Ceausescu, of Khrushchev after Stalin, and even of Deng Xiao Ping after Mao, Gorbachev declared a perestroika, an open season to criticize his own predecessors. Let a hundred flowers bloom! Let the whole nation rise up to blame certain others for the ills of the system.

Soon, however, Gorbachev's role in transforming the Soviet Union out of existence (for which he was given the Nobel Prize and was named Man of the Decade by *Time* magazine) was dramatically reassessed by former British prime minister Margaret Thatcher, who had prominently endorsed Gorbachev's glasnost in the 1980s. Now she conceded that "the role of Mikhail Gorbachev, who failed miserably in his declared objective of saving Communism and the Soviet Union, has been absurdly misunderstood."[7]

Few looked back to speculate about how they had been so misled. Those details suddenly became nothing but an arcane footnote in the history of foreign policy.

"NEW" RUSSIAN DEMOCRACY

On the evening of Christmas Day 1991, the flag of the Soviet Union was lowered from the Kremlin for the last time. The next day, the Soviet Union was dissolved, and Russia's imperial tricolor banner was raised again over the Kremlin. The world watched in amazement as the Russians, armed with only a fierce desire for freedom, brought down one of the most repressive forms of government known in history. A few days later, Boris Yeltsin, president of the Soviet republic of Russia, along with the presidents of Ukraine and Belarus, signed a treaty creating the Russian Commonwealth of Independent States.

Millions of Russians began donating money to resuscitate another Russian symbol: the Cathedral of Christ the Savior, built in the nineteenth century in thanks to God for Russia's victory over Napoleon. The NKVD had dynamited it in 1931 as part of Stalin's war against religion that razed fifty thousand churches and killed over three times that number of clergy.

The Soviet Union's spectacular collapse made the Kremlin a hit in the West, for a time. Public opinion in Russia was a horse of another color. Suddenly allowed to speak freely, Russians spent most of their time venting their pent-up anger and frustrations. Everybody began fighting everybody else and waiting for another miracle to occur.

The privileged Moscow *nomenklatura* decided that Russia's president, Mikhail Gorbachev, was a loser. They appealed for help to the KGB—the traditional Russian way out of a Kremlin power struggle. On June 22, 1991, the chairman of the KGB, Vladimir Kryuchkov, informed the Soviet parliament that Russia was on the brink of catastrophe. According to "reliable" KGB sources, he explained, the CIA was drawing up plans for the pacification and even occupation of the Soviet Union.

Seemingly coincidentally, Kryuchkov 's speech was "clandestinely" videotaped and broadcast on Russia's television that same evening. Two months later, Kryuchkov launched a coup d'état against Gorbachev in

Moscow. On August 18, 1991, following a pattern similar to that which ousted Nikita Khrushchev, the KGB arrested Gorbachev at his summer residence in the Crimea and took over the Kremlin. Thousands of unarmed citizens defended the building. An insurgent tank switched sides. Boris Yeltsin, standing on its top, passionately appealed to the people of Moscow to preserve the "Soviet order."

That speech, televised worldwide, was the birth certificate of a new Soviet star. Boris Yeltsin, who had been expelled from the Communist Party in July of 1990, asked in front of international TV cameras that the Communist Party of the Soviet Union be banned and its properties confiscated. People cheered.

Then and there the Communist Party expired, and no one missed it. Until Lenin came along, Russia had never had a significant political party anyway. Even after Lenin, the Communist Party had been merely the tool of the autocrat, not a forum for political competition, as the term "party" implies in the West.

EVOLUTION TOWARD INVOLUTION

The first freely elected president in Russia's history, Boris Yeltsin, was not only as different from his predecessor, Mikhail Gorbachev, as two human beings could be, he also had divergent political goals, tactics, and strategies. Gorbachev was convinced, and continues to be convinced to this day, that he could have saved the bankrupt Soviet Union by persuading the West to finance his "Marxist society of free people." Therefore, he geared all his efforts toward cozying up to the United States and its Western allies.

Yeltsin, on the other hand, believed that making a name for himself in the West was a dangerous game with potentially fatal consequences. Therefore, he decided it would be wise for him to ignore the United States and its Western allies for a while and focus on his own image as a jolly tsar who was as Russian as vodka. His fondness for the bottle even turned out to be a plus.

Since the sixteenth century's Ivan the Terrible, Russia had been a *samoderzhavie*, its own historical form of totalitarian autocracy in which a feudal lord rules the country with the help of a political police loyal only to him. That is what Russia's new president also wanted to do.

Boris Yeltsin began the rise to his new power by distancing himself from communism, even though, as a Communist Party and Politburo member, he had served in its top ranks. His post-Soviet biographies stressed his engineering career and how he "mastered twelve construction worker skills (stonemason, carpenter, driver, glazier, plasterer, etc.), a unique achievement for a young college graduate." He was stretching the truth in saying that he had joined the Communist Party late, more as an engineer than as a politician, at the advanced age of thirty-one and as "vice chairman of the Construction Department, then secretary on construction issues of the Central Committee of the CPSU." He lied. But most Russian autocrats do that.

Yeltsin began to build his own samoderzhavie. First, he renamed the Soviet PGU (Pervoye Glavnoye Upravleniye, or First Chief Directorate of the KGB) with a more American-sounding name, Central Intelligence Service (Tsentralnaya Sluzhba Razvedki, or TsSR), so as to pretend that it was a new Westernized organization. TsSR's new chief, Yevgeny Primakov, was a former KGB general whose first intelligence cover had been as a journalist in the West and, later, chief foreign intelligence advisor to Iraq's Saddam Hussein. During the first Iraq war, Primakov ferried messages between Gorbachev and Saddam Hussein, who had long been a Soviet client.

Next, Yeltsin began "rehabilitating" the KGB by appointing a new KGB chief, Vadim Bakatin, and pretending that the KGB had become a democratic organization. Bakatin was an undercover KGB officer and a former head of the Soviet Ministry of Interior in charge of the Soviet gulag system and internal repression. A new glasnost campaign for Western consumption portrayed Bakatin as an educated admirer of all things American; a fan, in his youth, of the Beatles and Elvis Presley; and—miracle of miracles—of American jazz. "My favorite album is *Blue Pyramid*," Bakatin told the *New York Times* in November 1991.

David Wise, an American journalist who visited Bakatin at KGB headquarters, wryly noted that a statue of the KGB founder, Felix Dzerzhinsky, still stood guard over the new chairman's reception area.[8]

That there was in fact no "new" KGB was suggested in an interview with Bakatin's personal spokesman, KGB General Alexei Karbainov, by the *New York Post* on November 25, 1991. In a long conversation with American journalist Uri Dan in his office at the Lubyanka, General Karbainov promised that the "new" KGB would help American authorities learn the whole truth about the "old" KGB.

What about Julius and Ethel Rosenberg? Dan asked. "I have no material about them," Karbainov shot back, "no files. Nothing about the alleged nuclear spying." Dan then recalled that Nikita Khrushchev had admitted in his memoirs that the Rosenbergs had "significantly" helped the Soviet Union build its first A-bomb and asked, "If you had material about the Rosenbergs, would you provide it?" Feigning incomprehension, Karbainov brusquely changed the subject.[9]

During Pacepa's years at the top of the KGB community, General Sakharovsky used to discuss the Rosenbergs quite proudly. According to Sakharovsky, by going to the executioner without confessing that they had become KGB agents, the Rosenbergs had laid the groundwork for "our all-important anti-American movements." Soon after that, left-wing peace demonstrations became big business for the KGB, worldwide.

On January 24, 1992, Yeltsin abolished the KGB and created a "new, democratic organisation" called the Ministry of Security of the Russian Federation (Ministerstvo Bezopasnosti Rossiyskoy Federatsii, or MB) run by another former KGB general, Viktor Barannikov.[10] In October 1993, when the Russian parliament rebelled against Yeltsin, the MB stormed the parliament building with artillery and arrested Yeltsin's antagonists. After thus "resolving" the Russian parliamentary crisis, Yeltsin ordered the MB to attack the Chechen rebels. The towns of Grozny and Pervomayskoye, where the rebels had taken refuge, were razed in a war that cost over 30,000 lives.

In December 1993, Yeltsin abolished the MB by *ukase*, or Russian government edit. That was another lie. It was merely rebaptized as the Federal Counterintelligence Service (Federalnaya Sluzhba Kontrrazvedki, or FSK). Former KGB General Nikolai Golushko was appointed director of the "new" organization until March 1994, when he was replaced by another old KGB hand, Sergey Stepashin.[11]

A 1993 FSK report to Yeltsin claimed that foreign secret services were now busy trying to flood the Russian market with poisonous alcohol, bad cigarettes, fake money, drugs, and pornography, echoing the same lies Stalin and all his successors had used to drum up fear and nationalist paranoia against the Western enemy. "The objective of these foreign services," added that report, was also "to infiltrate disguised leaders of criminal organizations in Russia's power structures, and then to dictate conditions of trade relations."[12]

On April 3, 1995, Yeltsin renamed the FSK as the Federal Security Service of the Russian Federation (Federalnaya Sluzhba Bezopasnosti v Rossiyskoy Federatsi) or FSB, and he appointed former KGB General Mikhail Barsukov to head the "new" organization.

Two days later, Yeltsin quietly gave the "new" FSB the same powers and duties the KGB had always had: the power to monitor political groups deemed a threat to the state, search homes and businesses, control all state secrets, carry out counterintelligence operations within the government and military, form businesses, infiltrate foreign organizations, conduct investigations, and run its own prison system.[13]

Most former Soviet states adopted identical patterns. Their "new" intelligence agencies made only superficial stabs at reorganization but never cut their ties to Russia's new KGB, now FSB. Belarus's political police didn't even bother to change its KGB name.

The final result? Lenin's secret police established in 1917 stayed solidly in place under their new brass nameplates. Over the years it had changed its name many times, from Okhrana to Cheka, to GPU, to OGPU, to NKVD, to NKGB, to MGB, to MVD, to KGB. Now it was called the FSB.

Boris Yeltsin will go down in history as among the founders of the first intelligence dictatorship in history.

THE PERIL OF CATCHING COLD

In the summer of 1996, Boris Yeltsin was elected Russia's president for a second time, but he was running the county through his political police, not a political party. Russia was never democratic, and that would not be its future. An ill-conceived privatization was underway to enable a small clique of predatory Russian insiders to plunder the country 's most valuable assets.

By 1999 the looting had become so outrageous that people attending auctions of state-owned businesses often carried banners with the slogan "privatizatsiya (privatization)=prikhvatizatsiya (grabbing)."[14] "They are stealing absolutely everything and it is impossible to stop them," explained Anatoly Chubais, the Yeltsin-appointed privatization tsar, who by that time was a billionaire who owned a good part of Russia's energy industry himself.[15]

Corruption from the looting of state assets penetrated every corner of the country, eventually creating a Mafia-style economic system that threatened the stability of all of Russia. In July 1998, the ruble plummeted by 75 percent of its 1997 value, short-term interest rates rose from 21 percent to 60 percent, and the stock market slumped by 60 percent of its value in the previous year. Petropavlovsk, the capital of Kamchatka, and a few other smaller towns lost electricity due to unpaid bills.[16] Yeltsin unsuccessfully tried to solve the crisis by sacking two prime ministers within six months: Viktor Chernomyrdin in March and Sergey Kiriyenko in August.

Facing economic chaos and civil disobedience, Yeltsin increasingly cut back on democratic experiments and governed through the traditional Russian reliance on the political police. According to Yevgenia Albats, a respected Russian intelligence expert and the author of a well-documented book about the KGB, "the Soviet Union, with a population of 300 million, had approximately 700,000 political police agents; Yeltsin's new 'democratic' Russia, with a population of only 150 million, has 500,000 Chekists. Where we once had one Chekist for every 428 Soviet citizens, we now have one for every 297 citizens of Russia."[17]

Yeltsin continued to build his samoderzhavie. In mid-1996, when General Barsukov's old affiliation with the KGB became too notorious, Yeltsin replaced him with a less-known KGB officer: General N. D. Kovalev. In August 1998, Yeltsin appointed the chief of his espionage service, former KGB General Yevgeny Primakov, as prime minister and gave him the task of transforming Russia into a "managed democracy," whose "democratic institutions" were to become "representative of the state: loyal, obedient, and indebted to those who have chosen them." The Kremlin even invented a word for this form of democracy: dogovorosposoniye, meaning, roughly, "deal-cutting."[18]

Soon, however, Yeltsin realized that the former chief of Russia's foreign intelligence service, who had also become an oligarch, intended to run for the Kremlin himself. Therefore, in May 1999, Yeltsin fired Primakov and appointed in his place a more devoted KGB officer: General Sergey Stepashin. He had spent most of his life conducting counterrevolution operations in remote parts of the country for the KGB.

By that time the Kremlin was reporting more and more often that Yeltsin was suffering from a "cold." Colds have historically proved lethal for the country's rulers. (Former presidents Konstantin Chernenko and Yuri

Andropov were dead within weeks after catching "colds.") The Kremlin soon acknowledged that in fact Yeltsin had the "flu," which later proved a euphemism for multiple bypass heart problems.

Medical technology since the fall of Soviet Union had improved, for the leadership at least. Yeltsin, however, caught one more "cold," reported at first as a post-sauna chill, which turned into a two-month bout of pneumonia. Another presidential stagnation set in.[19] One Moscow newspaper speculated that a putsch against the ailing Yeltsin was in the making.[20] Fearful of overthrow, and of having to go down in history as having dismembered the Soviet Union, the weakened Yeltsin put his whole fate in the hands of his political police.

General Pacepa's former office in the Soviet bloc sported a banner that said, all in upper case letters, "CAPITALIST ESPIONAGE REPORTS HISTORY. WE MAKE IT." Russian intelligence services are not defensive in operation, as Western intelligence services are. Its tsars, communist or otherwise, use their intelligence services to run the country and to elevate themselves. Yeltsin followed that rule. In August 1999, he sacked Stepashin and appointed a new prime minister: Vladimir Putin, a twenty-five-year KGB veteran who spoke two foreign languages and had a more diversified experience. Having spent the last eight years of his intelligence career in East Germany, his KGB activity was little known in Russia.

In 1999 Pacepa and his wife, an American writer, visited the bleak Stasi headquarters containing the Soviet–East German "House of Friendship," a KGB unit, in Dresden, East Germany, to see where Putin was "Europeanized." According to the Gauck Commission—a special German panel that researched the files of the Stasi headed by Lutheran minister Joachim Gauck, who later became president of unified Germany (2012–2017)—Putin was always surrounded by Stasi guards with machine guns and police dogs. KGB propaganda by contrast implied that Putin's experience had been that of a latter-day Peter the Great, touring the parlors and ballrooms of gay Paree. In reality, Putin's job was to secretly recruit East German engineers as KGB agents and send them to the West to steal modern technologies.

The combination of Putin's personal ambition, Yeltsin's health collapse, and the latter's likely fear of being accused of dismembering the Soviet Union may have convinced the weakened Yeltsin to put his entire fate in the hands of his Russian political police.

A KGB COUP IN THE KREMLIN

With the abolition of the Communist Party and the opening of the borders, Russia has been transformed in complex ways. The barriers the Kremlin spent seventy years erecting between the Soviet Union and the rest of the world, as well as between individual Russians, might have come down. When the Soviet Union collapsed, Russia had a unique opportunity to cast off that peculiarly Russian instrument of power, its political police, the Okhrana, created by Ivan the Terrible in the sixteenth century. The Russian people proved as yet not ready to seize that opportunity.

On New Year's Eve 1999, our old KGB counterparts must have been chortling in their graves when KGB Colonel Vladimir Putin installed himself as Russia's president at the end of a quiet KGB coup. Boris Yeltsin, the first freely elected president in the history of Russia, announced his forced resignation before a gaily decorated Christmas tree and a blue, red, and white Russian flag with a golden eagle. "I understand that I must do it and that Russia must enter the new millennium with new politicians, new faces, new intelligent, strong, energetic people."[21]

Yeltsin then announced that he had signed a decree "on the execution of the powers of the Russian president," stating that under Article 92 Section 3 of the Russian Constitution, the function of the Russian president shall be performed by Vladimir Putin starting from December 31, 1999.[22] Putin then signed another decree pardoning Yeltsin, who had been accused of massive bribery schemes, "for any possible misdeeds" and granting him "total immunity" from being prosecuted (or even searched and questioned) for "any and all" actions committed while in office. Putin also gave Yeltsin a lifetime pension and a state dacha.[23]

Quid pro quo, most of the Western media noted. In reality, it was a quiet KGB palace coup.

Now it was back to the future. In keeping with Stalinist traditions, Russia's schoolbooks released in September 2000 said of the unknown Putin: "This is your president, the one responsible for everything in this country.... He is not afraid of anything. He flies in fighter planes, skis down mountains and goes where there is fighting to stop wars. And all the other presidents of other countries meet with him and respect him very much." On December 31, 2000, the anniversary of his coup, Putin resurrected Stalin's national anthem with new lyrics by Sergey Mikhalkov, then eight-seven, who had been Stalin's official lyricist.

Yelena Bonner, the widow of Nobel Peace Prize–winner Andrey Sakharov, called the revived Soviet anthem a "profanation of history." Putin disagreed: "We have overcome the differences between the past and the present."[24] In his own way, Putin was right. During the Cold War, the KGB was a state within a state. Now the KGB—rechristened FSB—is the state.

CHAPTER 9

AS RUSSIAN AS THE BALALAIKA

By June 2003, some six thousand former KGB and Red Army officers held important positions in Russia's central and regional governments. Among them: Vladimir Putin, president of Russia; Dmitri Medvedev, prime minister; Sergey Ivanov, defense minister; Vladimir Osipov, head of the Presidential Personnel Directorate; Viktor Vasilyevich Cherkesov, chairman of the State Committee on Drug Trafficking[1] and former chief of the KGB's infamous Directorate V, in charge of crushing internal dissidence.[2] That year, Sergey Lavrov, KGB Academy graduate and now Russia's minister of foreign affairs, was named Russia's ambassador to the United Nations and president pro-tempore of the UN Security Council.

To Ted Koppel of ABC television, Putin explained that he needed the KGB and Red Army men to root out graft. "I have known them for many years and I trust them. It has nothing to do with ideology. It's only a matter of their professional qualities and personal relationship."[3] This was a half-truth. Filling governmental positions with undercover intelligence officers was as Russian as the Kremlin's onion domes. Until 1913, Roman Malinovsky edited *Pravda*. He was recruited by the Okhrana as an undercover agent while serving a jail term for theft and burglary. Erasing his criminal record, the Okhrana infiltrated him into Lenin's Communist Party, where he gradually rose to the position of chairman of the Bolshevik faction in the Duma.

The entire Soviet bloc was run with deep-cover intelligence officers. In the 1970s, during a meeting held with foreign trade officials, Romanian prime minister Ion Gheorghe Maurer whispered into Pacepa's ear: "Do you know what would happen if you smeared shit over every undercover officer of yours in this building?" Maurer did not wait for an answer: "This whole huge damn place would stink of shit from cellar to attic!"

In 1978, a couple of weeks after Pacepa was granted political asylum by President Jimmy Carter, Romania unleashed the greatest political purge in its communist history. The Western media reported the event widely. Ceausescu demoted four Politburo members, fired one third of his cabinet, and replaced twenty-two ambassadors, all deep-cover intelligence officers whose military documents and secret pay vouchers Pacepa had regularly signed off on.

A new Cold War began to unfold between KGB-run Russia and the West just minutes after the Aug. 8, 2008, opening ceremony of the Beijing Olympics, at which world leaders, including President George W. Bush, had gathered. Russian tanks rolled across the Russian border into Georgia. "War has started," Putin announced. With a straight face, he claimed that the government of Georgia was harassing Russian "peacekeepers" in the breakaway Georgian region of South Ossetia. The Kremlin, he said, was pledged to "protect the lives and dignity of Russian citizens, no matter where they are located,"[4] and therefore Russia must commandeer Georgia.

On Sept. 11, 2002, hordes of KGB officers gathered at the Lubyanka, the infamous headquarters of the newly renamed FSB, shockingly to celebrate the 125th birthday of Feliks Dzerzhinsky—the mass killer who had created the Soviet political police. (They did not gather in sympathy with the American tragedy of the previous year.) At the event, KGB chairman Vladimir Semichastny, Pacepa's former colleague, groused to the gathering: "I think a goal was set to destroy the KGB, to make it toothless."[5]

Official Russian propaganda photographs had depicted President Putin posing as a "Tarzan," with a knife under his belt or a Kalashnikov in his hand for years. On September 11, 2014, another clutch of former KGB officers gathered at the Lubyanka. They celebrate this date every year. But that year President Putin also announced the resurrection of an elite Interior Ministry special forces unit, using Stalin's title for it, the Dzerzhinsky Division.

This must raise a question. Is it a pure coincidence that the terrorist attack on the United States on September 11, 2001, which killed almost three thousand people (and the attack that killed U.S. Ambassador Christopher Stevens and three other Americans in Benghazi on September 11, 2012) took place on the birthday of Feliks Dzerzhinsky, the founder of the Cheka, which is now celebrated every year in Russia? Putin's policies, his uses of terrorism and war, can only make one suspect his hand.

Intimidating Putin's enemies through political killings and Nazi-style invasions of foreign countries are other reasons to suspect the KGB's hand in the bloody September 11 and Benghazi attacks. In 2006, six years after defecting to the United Kingdom, former Russian intelligence officer Alexander Litvinenko told the West that he had brought Abu Musab Al Zarqawi to Russia to be trained as a terrorist by the KGB/FSB in 1996–97[6] and that he had learned that Zarqawi had formed al-Qaeda in Iraq (AQI)—now called ISIS. Former KGB officer Konstantin Preobrazhensky, who defected to the U.S. in 2006 and is a regular guest on Voice of America, testified that Litvinenko "was responsible for securing the secrecy of Al-Zarqawi's presence in Russia while he was trained by FSB instructors."[7]

The revelation that Al Zarqawi was a secret KGB/FSB operative has been ignored by our politicians—but not by the Kremlin, which savagely murdered Litvinenko with Polonium-210, a radioactive element used as a neutron trigger for nuclear weapons, in retaliation for his disclosures. In 2007 the United Kingdom called for Russian citizen Andrey Lugovoy (a former KGB officer) to be extradited to the UK on charges of murdering Litvinenko. Russia declined. Lugovoy overnight became a member of the Russian Duma, thus receiving parliamentary immunity.

In 2008, a new cold and potentially bloody war was in the making. Putin invaded Georgia.[8] In February 2014, Putin then annexed Crimea while denying that "democratic Russia" had anything to do with the unmarked, masked armed forces trying to ignite civil war in Ukraine, which caused the Ukrainians to refer to them sarcastically as "Martians."[9] The gunmen were identified by U.S. experts to be Russian Special Forces.

The Ukrainian government irrefutably proved the day after the event that Russian separatists, armed and trained by Russian foreign intelligence, had shot down Malaysia Airlines flight MH17 on July 17, 2014, killing all 298 on board. The Kremlin insinuated that the U.S. might have done it.[10]

Putin's Russia is as if postwar Germany were run by former Gestapo who openly deplored Nazi Germany's demise as a "national tragedy on an enormous scale," brought back "Deutschland Über Alles" as the national anthem, built dozens of new secret cities dedicated to nuclear bomb production, unleashed an Anschluss to rebuild the German-Austrian Empire, and invaded neighboring countries—Georgia and Ukraine. It is precisely how Hitler started World War II.

Meanwhile, all efforts to bring the former KGB to account for the millions of souls it murdered in Soviet Russia and abroad are met with howls of protest from Putin. Their fates are still locked up behind the walls of Lubyanka. Hundreds of thousands of former KGB officers, informants, and collaborators are still shielded by a veil of secrecy. "In Russia today, nobody is willing to recognize the horrendous crimes of the past," said Valeryia Dunayeva of the Russian human rights group Memorial. Her mother had been framed as a spy and shot; her father had died in a Siberian gulag after twenty-five years there of political imprisonment. "There are 17,000 of us who lost both parents in Moscow alone, but the authorities simply pretend we don't exist."[11]

KGB DEZINFORMATSIYA MOVES INTO THE KREMLIN

On August 12, 2000, the Kursk, one of Russia's newest nuclear submarines, sank to the floor of the Barents Sea, killing all 118 people on board. Russia's new president, Vladimir Putin, immediately deployed KGB-style *dezinformatsiya* to minimize the political damage by keeping the disaster secret or denying it as long as possible, minimizing its damage, and—when the truth came out—blaming the enemy. At first Putin kept the disaster a secret, allowing him to finish his summer vacation at the beach. When the Western media reported on the disaster, Putin tried to minimize it by announcing that the crew of the submarine were still alive and that a special navy team was working to save their lives. Soon, the world learned that in fact the Russian navy had neither the technical means nor the expertise to carry out any such rescue operation. The Kremlin then alleged that the United States, its traditional enemy, might have caused the disaster. Russian Minister of Defense, former Soviet General Sergey Ivanov, claimed that on August 17, 2000, the Russian navy had intercepted an American submarine signal leaving the site of the Kursk's crash and suggested it might have collided with the Kursk.[12]

Several Western governments, realizing that Russia did not have the technical capability to rescue the Kursk, offered help. The Kremlin refused to accept it. Newspapers around the world accused the new Russian government of being "still in the grip of the morally outdated Soviet ideology" and failing to make "human lives the primary concern."[13] "The Russian elite's reflexes have not changed in the past 10 to 15 years," charged one.[14] One columnist made a direct appeal to Putin: "As Putin watches the crisis reach its nadir from his distant holiday home on the shores of the Black Sea, he must remember that his country is now a very different place from the oppressive and secretive one dominated by his communist predecessors. It is time the prime minister [sic] brought Russia in from the cold."[15]

Reluctantly, President Putin accepted a foreign offer of help. The first Norwegian divers reached the Kursk on August 20 and found no one alive, though the Kremlin, in order to calm public opinion, had just reported signs of life from the submarine. Lying was its first reflex.

In the fall of 2001, the Kursk was raised from the ocean floor by two Dutch salvage companies. Experts established that it sank due to a leak of hydrogen peroxide in the submarine's forward torpedo room, causing a torpedo warhead to explode that in turn triggered the explosion of a half dozen other warheads.

President Putin awarded the Order of Courage to all the deceased crew and made the submarine captain a Hero of the Russian Federation but never acknowledged the Russian avalanche of lies to cover up the disaster.

There is nothing unusual about this response. The use of *dezinformatsiya* to conceal and lie about killings and national calamities goes all the way back to the tsars. One day in 1839, a storm sank a fleet of boats crossing the Gulf of Finland from St. Petersburg to view an illumination display put on by Tsar Nicholas I at his summer residence of Peterhof. Marquis Astolphe de Custine (a visiting French nobleman who became famous after publishing his diary about his trip) wrote: "Today two hundred people are admitted to have been drowned; some say fifteen hundred, others two thousand.

No one will ever know the truth, and the papers will not even mention the disaster—that would distress the Czarina and imply blame of the Czar."[16]

The art of *dezinformatsiya* was also famously deployed in the Kremlin's handling of the Chernobyl disaster, 147 years after the unacknowledged fiasco at Nicholas I's fête. On April 26, 1986, an explosion ripped apart one of the four water-cooled nuclear reactors at the Chernobyl nuclear power plant in northern Ukraine. The official record as of today is that twenty people died fighting the fire, 135,000 others were evacuated, and an area within a radius of thirteen miles was declared a "forbidden zone."[17] In spite of its dimensions and its danger for all of Eastern Europe, Soviet president Mikhail Gorbachev kept the disaster a secret. Only when the Swedish government announced that it had detected fallout from the explosion did Gorbachev admit a "small" nuclear accident. But he said the reactor's core had immediately been sealed off with air-dropped cement.

Later, Eastern and Northern Europe began to notice significant radioactive contamination of their farm products. Only then did the West start to see through Gorbachev's disinformation campaign. It took many more years for the world to uncover that, in fact, eight tons of deadly radioactive material had escaped from the Chernobyl reactor, and an estimated 370,000 people had suffered various degrees of radiation.[18] In the end, continued Russian obfuscation may mean we may never learn the true dimensions of the disaster.

No wonder the first page of the KGB manual on *dezinformatsiya* proclaimed on its first page, all in upper case letters, "IF YOU ARE GOOD AT *DEZINFORMATSIYA*, YOU CAN GET AWAY WITH ANYTHING."

THE WEALTHIEST MAN ON EARTH

"I looked the man [Russian President Vladimir Putin] in the eye" and "I found him to be very straightforward and trustworthy," President George W. Bush said at the end of the 2001 summit meeting held in Slovenia. "I looked into Putin's eyes and I saw a stone-cold killer," stated former CIA director Robert Gates. Knowing the widely unknown Russian "science" of disinformation and its understudy, glasnost, could change night into day.

In our view, Colonel Vladimir Putin is a twentieth century Russian tsar. The position of a tsar is that of the owner of a country and its people. Putin has occupied Russia's throne for twenty-one years. Yet Russia's Constitution only allows a person to be president for a maximum two terms of four years. Putin has served three full tours as president and two as vice president and is now serving his fourth term as president.

During Putin's twenty-eight years in the Kremlin, his personal wealth has secretly risen from a few thousand Russian rubles to an estimated $200 billion, making Putin more than twice as wealthy as Microsoft's Bill Gates, with a fortune of $79.2 billion, once the world's richest known person but no longer.[19] It was certainly no coincidence that in 2002 Putin was able to buy Gerhard Schroeder, chancellor of the traditionally pro-American Federal Republic of Germany, who agreed to join Putin in opposing most U.S. foreign policy initiatives. It was no accident that in 2005, when Schroeder lost elections for his third term as chancellor, he became one of the top officials of Gazprom, a giant state-owned Russian company then headed by today's Russian Vice President Dmitry Medvedev. Each intelligence service has a limited budget. The published CIA budget for 2018 was $59.4 billion. Putin's intelligence budget for the same year was unlimited.

President Putin is the latest in the long line of Russian tsars who have upheld the tradition of lifetime rule by expropriating the country's wealth and killing all who try to stop him, dating back at least to the sixteenth century's Ivan the Terrible, who killed thousands of boyars and others, including Metropolitan Philip and Prince Alexander Gorbatyl-Shuisky, for the crime of refusing to swear an oath of loyalty to his eldest, infant son. The first freely elected president in the millennial history of Russia, Boris Yeltsin, tried to distance himself from the Soviet Union. Putin, who deposed Yeltsin in a coup d'état, does the opposite: he struggles to rebuild confidence in Soviet institutions, the only ones he has ever known. His long experience with the KGB "science" of *dezinformatsiya* put him into power and is what keeps him there.

On September 11, 2001, President Putin expressed sympathy to President George W. Bush for what he called "these terrible tragedies of the terrorist attacks."[20] He pretended to aid the United States by passing information to the FBI about two Russian immigrants in the U.S. who later perpetrated the 2013 Boston Marathon bombing. But these were gestures, not a break with Russia's anti-American past. In 2014, former KGB General Oleg Kalugin was charged with "high treason in the form of betraying a state secret" by Putin's chief military prosecutor for moving to the United States and publishing an autobiography[21] describing old KGB operations against the U.S.[22] Former KGB officer Lt. Colonel Alexander Litvinenko was assassinated for revealing Russia's key role[23] in forming ISIS and Al Qaeda in Iraq, starting with training Ayman Al-Zawahiri to conduct terrorist operations in Bosnia-Herzegovina during Yugoslavia's civil war, run out of Sofia, Bulgaria, which is now run by Rumen Radev, a member of the Communist Party until 1990 and backed in 2016 by the Socialist Party. As a result, the British have now forbidden any travel by Putin to the United Kingdom. For decades Bulgaria served as a primary surrogate for Soviet training and sponsor of terrorism. The Russians were playing both sides in the conflict, openly supporting the Serbs while covertly helping the Iranian-backed Muslims.[24]

Putin strikes traditionalist, "conservative" chords, preserving the worst parts of the old Soviet Union, its nativism and xenophobia. He speaks fondly about his years in the KGB,[25] asking the nation to understand that KGB "agents work in the interest of the state" and arguing for patience with them on the grounds that "90 percent" of all KGB intelligence was collected with the collaboration of ordinary citizens.[26] That kind of verbal spin may work with many as disarmingly honest. But it also ignores the brutal, lawless oppression solely at the whim of an autocrat that is the historical record of the Russian political police.

The *New York Times* dedicated its "Book Review" issue of November 30, 2014, to the publishing industry's reluctance to bring out judgmental books about Russian president Putin, in particular *Putin's Kleptocracy* by Karen Dawisha, a highly respected American scholar of Soviet and Russian politics. This book was rejected by one of the United Kingdom's most prestigious publishers, Cambridge University Press, for fear of retribution. The publisher explained to Dawisha: "The decision has nothing to do with the quality of your research or your scholarly credibility. It is simply a question of risk tolerance."[27]

Indeed, in post-Soviet Russia alone, over three hundred political figures and newsmen who dared publicly criticize President Putin have been assassinated.[28] The criminal tactics to consolidate power by Putin are the same as those used by Ceausescu. Each were educated at a military school in Moscow, and each supervised his country's secret police before becoming his country's president. Ceausescu was eventually executed during an upsurge of popular disgust. He clearly shares the traditional Russian faith in the political police over party politics as a means to power—as well as the traditional Soviet-style anti-Americanism.

CHAPTER 10

THE "DRAGON" OPERATION

For fifty-six years, most of the world has believed that President John F. Kennedy was murdered by America. Much of the world has been told that the CIA, FBI, right-wing businessmen, and the Italian Mafia were the main perpetrators. This is a lie, set off fifty-six years ago by the KGB's worldwide disinformation campaign called "Operation Dragon."[1] President John F. Kennedy was not killed by the American government. The lie that JFK was assassinated by the CIA or the FBI is the result of a concerted KGB disinformation operation to divert attention away from the KGB's extensive connections with Kennedy's killer, Lee Harvey Oswald. Oswald was a twenty-four-year-old American Marine infatuated with Marxism who defected to Moscow in 1959, returned to the U.S. four years later with a Russian wife given to him by the KGB, shot President Kennedy, and was arrested by the Texas police before being able to escape back to Moscow. In a letter Oswald sent to the Soviet embassy in Washington on July 1, 1963—a couple of weeks before killing President Kennedy—Oswald had asked for an "urgent " entrance visa for his wife and another one, "separatbly," (spelling as in the original text) for himself.[2]

In 1963, when President Kennedy was assassinated, Pacepa was a deputy director of Romania's espionage service, the DIE. On the night of November 22, 1963, a few hours after President Kennedy had been killed, the DIE's chief *razvedka* adviser asked the DIE management to put the DIE on "code C alert" and to order its *rezidenturas* abroad to report everything they could learn about Kennedy's assassination. All Soviet and Eastern European embassies in the U.S. and Western Europe had been instructed to take similar measures.

On the evening of November 26, 1963, Soviet foreign intelligence chief Aleksandr Sakharovsky unexpectedly landed in Bucharest, his first stop on a blitz tour of the main "sister" services to coordinate an intelligence effort to divert world attention away from the Soviet Union by focusing suspicion for the killing of President Kennedy on the United States itself.

Beating the Warren Commission Report to the stores by several weeks, the first book to be published on the Kennedy assassination was *Oswald: Assassin or Fall Guy?* by former German Communist Party member Joachim Joesten. Without providing any evidence whatsoever, it alleges that Oswald was "an FBI agent provocateur with a CIA background." It was in essence the KGB's own first public report on Kennedy's assassination for U.S. publication—and it became a bestseller.

The United Kingdom's MI6 later documented from highly classified documents smuggled out to England by the respected KGB defector Vasili Mitrokhin that Joesten's publisher, Carlo Aldo Marzani (codenamed Nord), had been funded via the KGB since before World War II to churn out pro-Soviet propaganda. In the 1960s alone, Marzani was subsidized by the Central Committee of the Soviet Communist Party to the then-quite-hefty tune of $672,000.

Joesten's book was dedicated to Mark Lane, an American leftist and one-time New York state representative who would soon publish a number of conspiracy theory books himself. Mark Lane's 1966 bestseller was entitled *Rush to Judgment*. In it he alleged that Kennedy was assassinated by a right-wing American group. Documents in the Mitrokhin Archive show that the KGB sent Mark Lane money at this time. According to KGB defector Oleg Gordievsky (former KGB station chief in London), a KGB operative, Genrikh Borovik, was in regular contact with him. Borovik was the brother-in-law of General Vladimir Kryuchkov, who in 1988 became chairman of the KGB and in August 1991 led the coup in Moscow aimed at restoring the Soviet Union.

The first review of Joesten's *Oswald: Assassin or Fall Guy?* was a rave that spread the sensational suggestion that Oswald must have been an agent of the FBI or CIA. Signed by Victor Perlo, a member of the Communist Party USA, it was published on September 23, 1964, in *New Times*, a KGB front widely distributed in several languages. At one time the *New Times* had been printed in communist Romania.

In a December 9, 1963, article, I. F. Stone, a prestigious American journalist, praised the Joesten book and speculated about why America might have wanted to murder its own president. Stone blamed the assassination on the "warlike Administration" of the United States that was trying to sell Europe a "nuclear monstrosity." Stone has been identified as a paid KGB agent, codenamed "Blin."

These big bestsellers generated scores of imitators as well as hundreds of wild-eyed articles and reviews. Most pushed far-fetched theories while studiously ignoring Soviet and Cuban involvement.

In 1967, New Orleans district attorney Jim Garrison arrested a man in his home district. Garrison accused this person of conspiring with U.S. intelligence agencies to murder Kennedy for his dovishness. The accused was acquitted in 1969, but Garrison kept promoting his story, first with *A Heritage of Stone* (Putnam, 1970) and later in *On the Trail of the Assassins* (Sheridan Square, 1988), one of the books that inspired Oliver Stone's movie, *JFK*.

Other titles such as Sylvia Meagher's *Accessories After the Fact: The Warren Commission, the Authorities, and the Report* (Vintage, 1976) accused reactionary elements in the Cuban exile community. Meagher suggested there may have been a "second Oswald" in line with the Oswald sightings that had begun to surface. One Richard H. Popkin even wrote a book entitled *The Second Oswald* (Avon, 1966), and Marina Oswald agreed to have her former husband's grave reopened to see who was buried there. It was Lee.

After the Senate's Church Committee released its report in 1976 showing that the CIA had been working with the Mafia and Cuban exiles on plans to assassinate Fidel Castro, a flood of new books began coming out to link those elements with the JFK assassination, such as Seth Kanthor's *Who Was Jack Ruby?* (Everest, 1978), Anthony Summers's *Conspiracy* (Paragon, 1980), and David E. Scheim's *Contract on America: The Mafia Murder of President John F. Kennedy* (Shapolsky, 1988, reprinted by Kensington).

Theories involving the CIA and other elements of the U.S. government were fueled by new material that began to be obtainable in the 1970s under the Freedom of Information Act, although those materials provided no particularly relevant facts to add to the Warren Commission Report. These theories continued to attract imaginative books such as Henry Hurt's *Reasonable Doubt* (Henry Holt, 1987), Robert J. Groden and Harrison Edward Livingstone's *High Treason: The Assassination of President John F. Kennedy: What Really Happened* (Conservatory, 1989), and Philip H. Melanson's *Spy Saga: Lee Harvey Oswald and U.S. Intelligence* (Praeger, 1990).

In the late 1970s, Edward Jay Epstein conducted his own investigation, published as *Legend: The Secret World of Lee Harvey Oswald* (Reader's Digest/McGraw Hill, 1978). This book introduced new and useful material on Oswald and was conscientiously documented but generally ignored by other assassination analysts. Epstein claimed to have interviewed over four hundred persons who had been, in one way or another, associated with Oswald. Among them were "about seventy Marines Oswald had served with in Japan and the Far East," most of whom "had never been previously interviewed by the FBI, or the Warren Commission." Epstein's book was centered around suspicions that Oswald had ties to Soviet (or Cuban) intelligence and provided significant new information showing that Oswald had indeed been manipulated by Moscow. Epstein's information strongly suggested that George de Mohrenschildt, the wealthy American oilman who had reportedly come from the old Russian nobility and who became Oswald's "best friend" after Oswald returned to the United States, was in fact Oswald's KGB "handler."

Like everyone else who has written about the JFK assassination, however, Epstein, too, lacked the inside intelligence background knowledge that would have helped him fit his bits and pieces together into a whole from which to come to a firm conclusion. His well-documented story is left hanging in midair.

Other books related to the JFK assassination provide useful new information but in varying degrees refrain from analysis. These include William Manchester's *The Death of a President: November 22–25, 1963* (Harper & Row, 1967), Robert L. Oswald's (with Myrick and Barbara Land) *Lee: A Portrait of Lee Harvey Oswald* (Coward-McCann, 1967), and Priscilla Johnson McMillan's *Marina and Lee* (Harper & Row, 1978). The latter book is badly flawed because of the author's unquestioning attitude toward everything Marina told her, much of which was not true. Similarly, Norman Mailer's *Oswald's Tale: An American Mystery* (Random House, 1995) was essentially based on information fed to him by the Soviets. Mailer concluded that Oswald probably acted alone, although there might have been some CIA and FBI involvement. Taking the opposite view was John Newman's *Oswald and the CIA* (Carroll & Graf, 1995), which conjures up a fictitious account of Oswald's involvement in CIA operations through extensively footnoted but only marginally relevant new U.S. government releases.

The popularity of books on the JFK assassination has encouraged all kinds of people to join the party to speculate based on their own backgrounds and perspectives. Many witnesses to the JFK assassination claimed to have heard more shots, seen more assassins, or observed different wounds than as stated in the Warren Commission report, even though the latter's forensic conclusions have repeatedly been declared accurate by responsible analysts. For example, a ballistics expert supplied the information that led to Bonar Menninger's *Mortal Error: The Shot that Killed JFK* (St. Martin's, 1992), which concluded that a Secret Service agent probably killed JFK by accident. Gaeton Fonzi's *The Last Investigation* (Thunder's Mouth, 1993) was written by a journalist who worked with a House committee and claimed to have "personal" knowledge of a CIA/Oswald link through investigations he conducted in places like Miami. Computer expert David S. Lifton wrote *Best Evidence: Disguise and Deception in the Assassination of John F. Kennedy* (Macmillan, 1980), in which, on the basis of his own examination of photographs, he concluded that JFK's wounds had been altered before he was buried, although no purpose for doing so was offered. Dr. Charles A. Crenshaw also wrote a book questioning the wounds, *JFK: Conspiracy of Silence* (Signet, 1992).

In 1993 journalist Gerald Posner published *Case Closed: Lee Harvey Oswald and the Assassination of JFK* (Random House). Posner's book does a good job documenting that the U.S. government was not involved in Kennedy's assassination. To a professional intelligence investigator, however, *Case Closed* leaves quite a few essential operational details entirely unanswered. The book, for instance, accepted the Soviet explanation for how Oswald "defected" to the Soviet Union without questioning two stamps in his passport—provided by Moscow—indicating that on October 9, 1959, Oswald took a flight to Helsinki from London's Heathrow Airport that was in fact fictitious; there was no direct flight from London to Helsinki on that day. Nor did Oswald's name appear on the passenger manifest of any other flight from Heathrow that day or on any flight arriving in Helsinki from other European cities within this travel window.

In 1964 the CIA drafted a set of questions for the Soviet government designed to elicit data from the Soviets about Oswald's defection to the Soviet Union and the procedures under which he had been processed and controlled during the two and a half years he had spent in that country. The draft was, however, rejected by the Warren Commission. A commission memorandum dated February 24, 1964, explained that, according to the State Department, the CIA's draft would have had serious adverse diplomatic effects and that the State Department "feels that the CIA draft carries an inference that we suspect that Oswald might have been an agent for the Soviet Government and that we are asking the Russian Government to document our suspicions."[3] Instead, the State Department proposed that the commission send to Moscow "a very short and simple request for whatever information the Russian authorities" had available on Oswald. The Warren Commission complied.[4] It also asked the Soviet Union for statements from Soviet citizens who might have met Oswald during his residence in that country, but none were ever provided. Later, in response to a request from the House Select Committee on Assassinations relayed by the State Department, the Soviet government "informed the committee that all the information it had on Oswald had been forwarded to the Warren Commission, a statement that the committee greeted with skepticism, based on the advice it had received from a number of sources, including defectors from the KGB."[5]

After the Soviet Union collapsed, substantial new evidence proving KGB involvement in killing President Kennedy came to light. The next chapters of this book deal with this new evidence.

HARD PROOF: YELTSIN'S DISINFORMATION

Ever since the glory days of the tsars, Russian leaders have always loved a good hoax. Joseph Stalin took the game a step further, inventing the elegant, Frenchified name of *dezinformatsiya* and turning deception into the most important weapon of Russian statecraft, as it still is today.

When carefully examined, disinformation can often reveal far more than was intended if the purpose for the cover-up can be deciphered. The tangle of threads can be unraveled.

Before embarking on our new look at the assassination of President Kennedy in light of the scattered details that have emerged in the more than fifty years since, it is most useful to review the significant revelations made by former Russian president Boris Yeltsin in Appendix B of his remarkable memoir entitled *The Struggle for Russia.*[6] In December 1991, at his last meeting with his predecessor Mikhail Gorbachev, Yeltsin says he received a huge treasure trove of ultra-secret KGB documents that had been passed down from Soviet leader to Soviet leader. From this material Yeltsin chose (i.e., was instructed) to publish a few of what he calls "relatively old and not especially hot documents" in order to show the "routine, bureaucratic side of the KGB's activity."

These three documents were directly related to the assassination of President John F. Kennedy. Though Yeltsin says he included them precisely because of their "mundane, ordinary tone," they turn out to be a revealing collection of disinformation. They purport to be highly secret letters and memoranda sent by KGB bosses to top levels of the Communist Party's Central Committee and International Department immediately after the assassination. All these documents, and Yeltsin's comments on them, point to various elements in the United States that are supposedly the real instigators behind the actions of Lee Harvey Oswald, the assassin of President John F. Kennedy. Oswald himself is merely described as a onetime supporter of the Soviet Union, Castro's Cuba, and the American Communist Party (CPUSA) who was diagnosed as suffering from psychiatric illness.

President Kennedy was shot at 12:30 p.m. on November 22, 1963, and Oswald, who was publicly known to have lived in the Soviet Union for a few years, was taken into custody a couple of hours later by the Dallas police as the suspected perpetrator. In Yeltsin's first letter, on the very next day, KGB chairman Vladimir Semichastny hastens to send the Central Committee of the Soviet Communist Party (CPSU) a nice, clean story about Lee Harvey Oswald, an American tourist who in 1959 applied to remain permanently in the Soviet Union, was given an apartment and a good job at a radio factory in Minsk along with a monthly stipend of seventy rubles, married a Russian girl, and then, as was usual in such cases, after a time decided to go back to the U.S., although a year later he was asking permission to return to the Soviet Union.

The above story is the kind of routine disinformation that the Soviets have passed out to everyone—in Russia and abroad—who was not privy to information about the KGB's earlier, very sensitive operational connection with Oswald. In addition, Semichastny includes the new disinformation that says that when Oswald visited the Soviet consulate in Mexico in October 1963 and asked for political asylum, he claimed that the FBI was persecuting him because he had been secretary of a pro-Cuba organization. The Cuban angle was not particularly stressed in early Soviet disinformation about the assassination, but as we shall see, it came to be considered an excellent way to downplay Oswald's well-known interest in communism by emphasizing his support for Fidel Castro and Cuban (rather than Soviet) communism.

We can point to a very different story of what Oswald was trying to accomplish on that trip to Mexico, documented in full in a book by co-author Pacepa published in 2007.[7] Any more recent information will be so identified and sourced.

During the summer of 1963, Oswald was in New Orleans, noisily promoting the Fair Play for Cuba organization, including getting into a fight with Cuban émigrés and being arrested for disturbing the peace. From jail he demanded an interview with the FBI, which complied but was mystified about why it had been called in. On September 25, Oswald left New Orleans by bus, traveling under the alias O. H. Lee. After accomplishing his mission for Nikita Khrushchev—killing the American president—he would need an escape route back to the Soviet Union, which he considered his new homeland. Since the Soviet embassy in Washington had been giving Oswald and his wife the runaround when they asked for visas, Oswald now hoped he would be able to fly from Mexico to Cuba and from there on to Moscow. He was not seeking asylum; he just wanted to go back home to Russia after accomplishing his heroic task for Russia's leader.

After arriving in Mexico City on September 27, Oswald immediately made several visits to the Cuban embassy, which refused to give him a visa unless he had a Soviet one. There is no evidence that he actually visited the Soviet embassy, although CIA coverage did show that he made one phone call from the Cuban embassy to the Soviet embassy, saying he would be right over to see "Comrade Kostikov." Found after Oswald's death were notes suggesting clandestine meeting arrangements in Mexico City and the draft of a later letter to the Soviet embassy in Washington complaining about his unsuccessful encounter with Comrade Kostikov, aka Valery

Kostikov, an officer of the KGB's Department Thirteen (assassinations). A disappointed Oswald departed Mexico on October 2 for the two-day bus trip back to Dallas.

It is also interesting to consider what Semichastny says at the end of his memorandum to the Central Committee, keeping in mind that it is allegedly still November 23 when he writes this. He recommends publishing an article in "a progressive paper in one of the Western countries" so as to expose the attempt by reactionary circles in the United States to remove the responsibility for the murder of Kennedy from the real criminals, whom he describes as "the racists and ultra right elements guilty of the spread and growth of violence in the United States." Significantly, in view of the fact that Oswald was still alive but was going to be shot dead at the Dallas police station the very next day by Jack Ruby, who had criminal and intelligence ties to communist Cuba, Semichastny adds that the article should illustrate the intent of "crazy men" related to the "provocateurs and murderers among counterrevolutionary Cuban émigrés to alter the foreign and domestic policies of the USA." (The reference to Cuba is a little confused since Cuban émigrés would not have been backing Oswald, who had been noisily supporting Castro's Cuba. No matter, however, because the point was simply to add another group of potential culprits behind the assassination.)

Then Yeltsin gives us the most fascinating disinformation tidbit of all. In Moscow, it would already have been evening before Soviet authorities received reports of the assassination and even later of Oswald's arrest. Nevertheless, on the very next day, November 23, KGB chairman Vladimir Semichastny not only promptly sends a message to the Central Committee with the above fictitious information about that nice young man Oswald, but he goes on to recommend immediately starting, in effect, a full-bore disinformation campaign designed to point the finger at elements the Soviets want the world to view as the real criminals behind the assassination.

Along with the other memoranda and comments related to the assassination published in Appendix B in Yeltsin's book, the above letter must be considered pure disinformation for consumption by American and other Western readers. As we intelligence professionals can attest, Semichastny would never have written such bald lies to the Central Committee. The Central Committee certainly already knew about Oswald and his radar information that had famously helped the Soviets bring down a CIA U-2 plane intruder on May 1, 1960. (Oswald had even bragged to the American embassy in Moscow that he had told the Soviets all he knew about radar and American U-2 planes. As a Marine he had served at Atsugi in Japan, with its U-2s, and at El Toro in California, with its sophisticated new radars.) Furthermore, the sender of one memorandum is given as "Semichastny's deputy, Zakharov." We know, and the Central Committee also certainly knew, that this is really General Aleksandr Sakharovsky. Sakharovsky would not have written to the Central Committee in alias. Yeltsin also gives the codename "Brooks" as the source of information claiming that Oswald had written a letter offering to help American communists organize for the CPUSA and for Cuba, but the offer was considered an FBI provocation. "Brooks" is identified in the memorandum as "a well-known American Communist figure and KGB agent," an unlikely indiscretion to describe a sensitive agent. In 1999, "Brooks" will be publicly identified in the Mitrokhin Archive as Jack Childs, an American communist who was indeed a KGB agent.[8] By the time Yeltsin's book was published, Childs was dead, having passed away on August 12, 1980, so no harm was done by Yeltsin's outing him.[9] The reference to "Brooks" is probably intended to reassure the FBI that Jack was indeed a trusted KGB agent. In fact, Jack was also a trusted FBI source, as the Soviets knew. (The complicated significance of this point will be clarified in another chapter.)

Compare that with what the *New York Times* reported from Dallas on the morning of November 23, 1963. Oswald was arrested the previous afternoon, charged with the murder of a policeman who had tried to stop him from escaping, then arraigned at 1:40 a.m. the following morning and charged with the murder of the president. The accused was described as a twenty-one-year-old leftist who had once lived in the Soviet Union and who currently worked at the Dallas School Book Depository, from where the shots had come that had killed the president. He was also identified as an adherent of the Fair Play for Cuba Committee but described as politically somewhat erratic.

Why should the KGB leadership know better than the Dallas police and the *New York Times* who was to blame for the assassination of the American president? It is even more remarkable that the KGB chairman so accurately anticipates Oswald's murder the following day by Jack Ruby, who was not a Cuban émigré but had Cuban connections.

The KGB clearly had no trouble finding an appropriate "progressive paper in one of the Western countries" in which to launch its disinformation campaign about the Kennedy assassination. The first attack came in an article early in 1964 in the communist-controlled British journal *Labour Monthly*. Written by editor R. Palme Dutt, the article states that "most commentators" have surmised the assassination to have been a coup staged by the "Ultra-Right or racialists of Dallas" by using a fall guy they then killed before he could spill the beans. The scenario is described as having "all the hallmarks of a CIA job" without providing any evidence whatsoever of that.[10] In early 1964 the first book on the assassination was published in the United States. Written by German communist Joachim Joesten's, it is entitled *Oswald: Assassin or Fall Guy?* And it was published by Carlo Aldo Marzani, a known KGB agent (codename NORD), who had been generously funded since before World War II for churning out pro-Soviet propaganda. Joesten's book also hewed to Semichastny's line by blaming the assassination on a conspiracy of right-wing racists, especially oil magnate H. L. Hunt. It describes Oswald as an "FBI agent provocateur with a CIA background" who was used and then murdered to prevent his giving evidence.[11]

Accusing the CIA—to this day the main adversary of Russian intelligence, with the FBI a close second—of assassinating President Kennedy became thereafter a worldwide theme song in a flood of disinformation books and articles. Yet as coauthor Woolsey can attest, the CIA never had any kind of operational connection with Oswald. Nevertheless, it is said even to this day that half of the American population believes the CIA was responsible for the Kennedy assassination. Such is the formidable power of disinformation once it takes hold in the popular imagination.

Further, Yeltsin quotes a "Zakharov" memorandum to the International Department of the Central Committee in which "Zakharov" alleges that some intelligence data identify "the ultimate organizer of the murder of President Kennedy" as a politically powerful group of Texas oil magnates. He adds that a Polish [sic] intelligence source reported in November 1963 that the real instigators of the assassination were three prominent oilmen from the southern U.S. named Richardson, Murchison, and Hunt. Also noted is information privately given to "Ward, a reporter for the *Baltimore Sun*" in early December at the meeting of a group of Texas financiers and industrialists headed by the millionaire

Hunt claiming that Jack Ruby "had proposed a large sum of money to Oswald for the murder of Kennedy."

The Texas oil magnates pop up frequently in post-assassination disinformation, most notably in a "Dear Mr. Hunt" letter dated "Nov. 8, 1963" and signed by "Lee Harvey Oswald." Copies of this letter were anonymously mailed out in 1975 to three conspiracy advocates in the U.S., accompanied by a note alleging that the FBI had the original. Oswald provocatively asks for "information concerning my position" and suggests discussing the matter "before any steps are taken by me or anyone else." The handwriting was authenticated by several Western experts. In 1999 the "Dear Mr. Hunt" letter was identified in the Mitrokhin Archive as a KGB fabrication.[12] We can even tell how the fabrication was done, based on information supplied by the defectors Lazló and Hanna Sulner, who had perfected a copy machine that seamlessly combined individual letters actually written by a target person. This machine was used by the Hungarians to compromise Cardinal József Mindszenty in 1948–1949 and was made available to the Soviets.[13]

In the end, Yeltsin's very secret KGB documents in Appendix B that were supposedly written just after the assassination of President Kennedy turn out to be much later concoctions. They were evidently composed in order to have Yeltsin bring a little new life into the old Soviet disinformation campaign to absolve Russia of any operational involvement with Lee Harvey Oswald or the assassination. The Yeltsin documents also add a few new twists, mainly by directing somewhat more attention toward Cuban affairs.

THEY KNEW

By at least April 1963, the KGB had to face up to the probability that it might not be able to prevent Lee Harvey Oswald from going ahead with his idée fixe that he had to assassinate President Kennedy. Oswald knew that Nikita Khrushchev, the leader of Oswald's paradise and new home, the Soviet Union, had entrusted him with that task, and he was confident he could pull it off. In April he had demonstrated to the KGB officers in Mexico how carefully and successfully he had planned to take a shot at General Edwin Walker on April 10 without leaving any telltale evidence, and he was certain he could do just as good a job against Kennedy.

By this time, however, the KGB and the Soviet Union's Communist Party leaders realized that Khrushchev's crazy ideas were giving their country a terrible reputation. In October 1962, he had lost face before the world by backing down over the Cuban Missile Crisis and when the Soviet Union was named as the murderer of two Russian émigrés at the Bogdan Stashinsky trial in West Germany. Another false step by the hot-headed Khrushchev, and there might be nuclear war. By at least April 1963, rumors were afloat that Politburo ideologue Mikhail Suslov was leading a revolt to oust Khrushchev and replace him with Leonid Brezhnev.[14]

For its part, the KGB's disinformation experts began planning what to do about Oswald if he should resist all efforts to change his mind. At home the Soviets might have staged their usual fatal hunting or automobile accident, but they could not risk attempting such a solution in the United States. Apparently the next best choice was to divert public attention away from any Russian contact with or interest in him. Fidel Castro was brought into the picture and agreed to help focus Oswald's enthusiasm for communism more toward Cuba than as before toward Russia. In the process, Oswald might even forget about what Khrushchev had asked him to do.

On April 13, just before Oswald traveled to Mexico to show the KGB what a good shot he was, he had been visited for the last time by his best friend and mentor, George de Mohrenschildt. De Mohrenschildt was actually a KGB illegal officer assigned to help Oswald get settled in the United States, but he was evidently not aware of Oswald's assassination assignment. Oswald showed off the guns (rifle and pistol) that he had just received at the post office box he had opened in alias, and his wife took his picture with them. De Mohrenschildt must have used his own communications channel to tell the KGB about this alarming visit, because on April 19 he and his wife suddenly, without even saying goodbye to the Oswalds, packed up and left Dallas for Haiti, where they had previously lived.

Sometime between April 14 and April 24 (when there is no other record of his whereabouts), Oswald took a bus trip to visit the KGB in Mexico City. On his September 1963 bus trip to Mexico City, he told fellow passengers that on an earlier trip he had stayed at the Hotel Cuba. After the assassination a chambermaid recognized Oswald from a photograph as a previous guest at that hotel.[15] Otherwise, no facts are available about this April trip. In any case, Oswald certainly alarmed the KGB by describing his shot at General Walker and showing off the photographs of himself with his guns.

On April 24, Oswald sent his wife and child off to live with their kindly and unwitting friend Ruth Paine in the Dallas suburb of Irving. That same day he caught a bus for New Orleans, where he moved in with his aunt and started to organize some pro-Cuban activities.

The most serious problem for the Soviets was what to do if Oswald should pull off the unthinkable and actually assassinate the American president. Everyone knew President Kennedy would soon be visiting Dallas, the home of his vice president, and it eventually became public knowledge that the visit would take place on November 22, 1963.

This presented a problem way over the heads of Oswald's usual case officers. It was high time for the KGB leadership to call upon its top disinformation experts. Normally they could have easily published some kind of fake news in a Calcutta newspaper and gotten it reprinted in Western Europe and the United States. But an attempted assassination of the president of the United States called for much more sophisticated planning. Knowledge of this top-secret dilemma obviously had to be kept extremely tight, perhaps limited to KGB chief Yuri Andropov, Communist Party ideologue and Brezhnev supporter Mikhail Suslov, and CPSU International Department chairman Boris Ponomarev, although Cuban leader Fidel Castro and CPUSA chairman Gus Hall would need to be brought in to a certain extent for their support. If the worst should indeed happen, the Soviets would have to be prepared to stage dramatic and convincing scenarios before gullible and carefully selected audiences who would need to convince the world that the neither the Soviet Union nor Cuba had any current connection with Lee Harvey Oswald.

Let us look chronologically at what happened on November 22, 1963.

First we have Florentino Aspillaga. He was a radio intercept officer with the Cuban intelligence service. His regular job was to monitor CIA transmissions from a communications hut on the shore near Havana. At about 9:30 that morning, he received a coded message to call his headquarters, which he then did from a secure phone. He was ordered to stop tracking the CIA, to listen instead to transmissions from Texas, and to report anything of interest back to headquarters. Two or three hours later, he picked up amateur radio bands reporting that President Kennedy had just been shot, and he reported this back to his headquarters. Kennedy was shot at 12:30 p.m. Dallas time, which would have been 1:30 p.m. Havana time. Aspillaga defected in Vienna in 1987 but was afraid to tell anyone about this incident, although he included it in his personal memoirs written soon thereafter when he came to the United States. He later recounted it to the CIA's authority on Cuba, Brian Latell, commenting simply: "Castro knew. They knew Kennedy would be killed." This did not become public knowledge until 2012, when Latell published it in his book *Castro's Secrets*, based mainly on interviews with Cuban defectors. Latell describes Aspillaga as "the most knowledgeable Cuban defector ever to change sides.[16]

Next we must take a look at Fidel Castro himself. On this day he was at his Varadero beach house, where he was hosting a luncheon for his distinguished foreign visitor Jean Daniel, the lead correspondent for the Paris weekly *L'Express*. Daniel had been in Cuba for several weeks and had spent the past two days talking to Fidel about politics between the United States and Cuba. Present at the beach house were Daniel, his wife, Fidel Castro, and nine or ten other Cubans. They were all sitting around a casual table when the phone rang and Fidel answered. It was Cuba's figurehead president calling with preliminary news of the assassination. Everyone present heard Fidel cry out: "¿Como? ¿Un atentado?" (What? An assassination attempt?) Fidel told his guests the news and called it an "amazing coincidence." When it was soon thereafter learned that the president was dead, Fidel remarked: "They will have to find the assassin quickly, otherwise you watch and see, they will try to blame us." The writer Brian Latell learned all of this later from Daniel, who said that his wife had thought Fidel seemed genuinely shocked. Latell commented that Fidel's remark about being blamed was strange, since at that time Oswald's Marxist and Cuban connections had not yet been made public. Daniel would later publish several articles in various French periodicals describing this scene.[17] This whole scenario had clearly been carefully planned in order to demonstrate to the foreign visitors that Fidel Castro had nothing to do with the assassination and was taken completely by surprise when he learned the news. Daniel was undoubtedly selected to be the honored guest at the luncheon because he would be sure to write articles for publication in Europe about what he had personally witnessed.

But the truly most amazing stage performance taking place that day involved the influential American communist Morris Childs, who had been in Moscow since November 1, 1963, on his annual trip for the American Communist Party (CPUSA) to discuss politics and funding with Soviet party (CPSU) leaders.[18] On November 22, as soon as news of the assassination started coming in, Soviet leaders in obvious consternation began talking to Morris about it, asking for his views on possible causes and advice on how the Communist Party should react.

International Department chairman Boris Ponomarev called Morris into his office and was asking about the kind of person Lyndon Johnson was when panic-stricken subordinates burst in and excitedly started telling in Russian about Oswald's arrest for the murder. They described Oswald as a former U.S. Marine who had defected to the Soviet Union, had attempted suicide, and had been judged by psychiatrists to be unbalanced. When Oswald had asked to go back to the United States, the Soviets were glad to be rid of him. When he later appeared at the Soviet embassy in Mexico and said he wanted to return to the Soviet Union via Cuba, the embassy asked KGB headquarters what to do and was told to brush him off. The Soviet embassy told Oswald it could not issue him a visa unless he had a Cuban visa, and the Cuban embassy cooperated by telling him he could not have a Cuban visa without showing that he had a Soviet one. Ponomarev's intruders said the KGB had now sworn to the Politburo and to the International Department that it had never at any time used Oswald as an agent or informant. (All of this was the standard disinformation story that would soon be spread around everywhere.)

When the intruders noticed Morris and asked what they should do with "this American here," Ponomarev told them to repeat their story for him in English. Remarkably, they just happened to speak English, and they did so. (Morris, who had been a loyal source of the FBI's since the early 1950s, always claimed he had made a great effort not to let the Soviets know he spoke Russian, but of course they did know from his background. He had spent the first nine years of his life in the Kiev area, where his family spoke Russian at home. Furthermore, the CPUSA had sent him as a teenager to Moscow to study at the Lenin School for foreigners, where he had also become an informant for the KGB's predecessor (OGPU) and was tutored by prominent Russians, notably Mikhail Suslov, who became his friend and mentor. (Coauthor Pacepa knew many Romanians who had attended the same school, and all came back speaking fluent Russian, even though the classes were given in their native languages.)

In short, it must be concluded that Ponomarev had planned this scenario well in advance, and he set Morris up for it. Indeed, Morris was impressed by the sincere concern and sympathy of all the Soviets he met with on this trip, and he was genuinely convinced that the Soviets had nothing to do with the assassination. When he got back to the United States on December 2, Morris immediately reported everything to the FBI, which transmitted the essence of it—it was described as being from an anonymous "source that has provided reliable information in the past"—to President Johnson, to a few other top administration leaders, and even in a secret summary to the Warren Commission, which had just been formed on November 29.

President Johnson was already familiar with earlier reporting from this source, whom he knew as a reliable FBI agent with access to top Soviet officials. The president and the FBI were enormously relieved to have confirmation that the Soviets had nothing to do with the assassination. The members of the newly formed Warren Commission were told not to look any more for a Soviet connection, and indeed they did not.[19]

We coauthors have, however, learned something quite different from these little stories. We have seen that Cuban leader Fidel Castro and the CPSU's International Department chairman Boris Ponomarev were well aware that Lee Harvey Oswald would try to assassinate President Kennedy on his visit to Dallas in November 1963, and they prepared elaborate disinformation scenes to convince gullible foreign visitors of their utter shock and surprise if and when the worst were to happen. Castro fed his fake news stories to a French writer with suggestions for who was behind the deed (Texas oilmen, Cuban émigrés, the CIA, the FBI), and Ponomarev fed his fake news to a high-ranking CPUSA representative, demonstrating that the Soviets had no connection whatsoever with the deed (though maybe President Johnson, rich Texans, or the CIA did).

Of course, we know that in fact Morris was a trusted FBI agent, so the disinformation was immediately disseminated to top levels of the U.S. government as the truth. What no Americans suspected, however, was that Ponomarev and other top Presidium members had long been aware that Morris was cooperating with the FBI. (We coauthors discuss elsewhere how we reached this firm conclusion.) The FBI and Morris himself never believed that the Soviet leaders knew all about his loyalty to the United States and cooperation with the FBI, and that was the key to the brilliant performance hosted by Ponomarev. On November 22, 1963, the Soviet Union truly pulled off a hugely successful disinformation show, one that would absolutely convince the top levels of the American government that the Soviet Union bore no responsibility whatsoever for the assassination of President Kennedy.

The American population and the world would get the message from eminently reliable and respected sources. Nuclear war would not erupt from either West or East. Behind the scenes, Suslov and the Politburo could work to get rid of that madman Khrushchev and put Leonid Brezhnev in the driver's seat.

As previously noted, on October 12, 1964, Nikita Khrushchev was recalled from his vacation, arrested at the Moscow airport, and forced to resign, giving way to Leonid Brezhnev as Communist Party leader.

THE CHILDS BROTHERS

It must finally be acknowledged that with Morris Childs and his brother Jack, the Soviet Union pulled off a brilliant disinformation operation, one that still distorts all efforts to analyze the assassination of President Kennedy. Who were these men, and why in all the thousands of books and articles written about the assassination is there hardly any mention of them?

Here we need not recount the whole story of the Childs brothers' remarkable lives. It has been well told in John Barron's book *Operation Solo: The FBI's Man in the Kremlin* (Regnery, 1996).[20] Briefly, both Morris Childs (1902–1991) and Jack Childs (1907–1980) were longtime, trusted members of the American Communist Party (CPUSA), Morris an overt and senior member responsible for policy and Jack an underground member responsible for obtaining the money Moscow sent through the KGB to support the CPUSA.

After World War II, the CPUSA went through a rough period of internal squabbles and U.S. government investigations, and it lost contact with and funding from the CPSU. The FBI seized the opportunity. In 1951 it recruited first Jack and then Morris, both of whom remained proud and loyal FBI agents for the rest of their lives. Beginning in 1958, Morris made lengthy annual trips to Moscow for meetings with leading members of the Soviet government to discuss political tactics and funding, and he also sometimes met with party leaders in other communist countries. As a KGB agent, Jack clandestinely retrieved the cash dollars that the CPSU sent through the KGB's Toronto and later New York stations to fund the CPUSA. Morris and Jack occasionally substituted for each other when one or the other was ill.

Until the end of their lives, both Childs brothers were highly regarded by both the American and the Soviet/Russian governments. In 1977, at a surprise seventy-fifth birthday party hosted by Soviet leader Leonid Brezhnev and attended by KGB chairman Yuri Andropov and about half of the Politburo, Brezhnev himself pinned an Order of the Red Banner medal on Morris's lapel, and Morris was told that Jack would also get the same medal when he next came to Moscow. Although Morris believed that the Soviets overestimated the work done by the CPUSA, he felt that the medal was also a personal tribute from the Soviet leadership.

In 1987 President Ronald Reagan ordered that the National Security Medal be awarded to Morris and posthumously to Jack, who had died in 1980. For security reasons, Morris received his award from Director William Sessions at FBI headquarters.

The FBI, and Morris and Jack themselves (and their wives, who sometimes traveled with them), always firmly believed no one ever knew that after the early 1950s the brothers had changed loyalties and were working for the FBI. Outside the FBI, no one was believed to know—not CPUSA leaders, not American government authorities, not the KGB, not the CPSU. American leaders knew them as reliable anonymous sources. Communists knew them as trusted colleagues both in the U.S. and Moscow and in other communist countries. When visiting communist countries, these loyal Americans were sometimes terrified that their secret might be discovered and that they would be arrested, but in fact they were always warmly welcomed everywhere as old friends.

Unfortunately, we coauthors must beg to differ. After very careful study, we have firmly concluded that the Soviet Politburo, as well as CPUSA chairman Gus Hall and later even Fidel Castro, had long known that the Childs brothers had been cooperating with the FBI since the 1950s. That sheds an entirely new light on how we must view the reporting from these very secret and reliable anonymous FBI sources, particularly with regard to the assassination of President Kennedy. Over the years, the reporting from the Childs brothers was in fact

Soviet-generated disinformation (although built around a kernel of truth for credibility's sake), and it distorted the conclusions reached by the FBI, by President Johnson, and by the Warren Commission, with ripple effects throughout Washington and much of the Western world.

The most authoritative evidence that top Soviets were aware of the Childs brothers' loyalty to the FBI comes from a close examination of the Mitrokhin Archive.[21] When reading this material, it must be remembered that the defector Vasili Mitrokhin had access only to documents in the archives of the KGB's PGU (Pervoye Glavnoye Upravleniya, the first or foreign intelligence chief directorate), roughly similar to the American CIA. He did not have access to material on cases run by any of the other KGB directorates or other elements of the Soviet government or to very sensitive cases known only to the KGB chairman. The Childs brothers were not a PGU case, although during the period 1958 to 1980, Jack and occasionally Morris did have clandestine contact with the PGU in connection with the transfer of CPSU funds to the CPUSA. The PGU knew that the brothers were working for CPUSA chairman Gus Hall and that in Moscow the CPSU's Politburo and International Department held them in high regard.

According to the Mitrokhin Archive, by at least 1974, the PGU officers in the United States had become suspicious of the Childs brothers, especially Morris. The Childs brothers had not suffered during the anti-communist witch hunts of the 1950s, nor had they been arrested for traveling on false passports the FBI was believed to have been aware of. (Indeed, we know from Operation SOLO that the FBI had provided them with false passports.) Furthermore, a 1967 U.S. Senate Judiciary report had named one of Morris's earlier aliases and mentioned his prewar links with Soviet intelligence. (From Operation SOLO we also know that the CPUSA sent Morris to study in Moscow from 1929–1932 and that he became an informant for the KGB predecessor OGPU during that period.) In March 1974, Vladimir Kazakov, the head of the PGU's North American department, reported these suspicions to KGB chairman Yuri Andropov and to the CPSU's Central Committee, saying that even though CPUSA chairman Gus Hall trusted Morris, the PGU suspected that Morris was "possibly being used by U.S. intelligence." The PGU also urged that Hall find a substitute for Jack, who was absent-minded and in poor health.

When there was no reaction to its letter, the PGU on May 8, 1974, had its chief, Boris Ivanov, personally meet in Moscow with Gus Hall in an effort to persuade him that the long involvement of both Childs brothers in secret work was increasingly putting PGU officers in danger of FBI surveillance. Ivanov suggested some other ways to transfer funds to the CPUSA. Hall said he had found a reliable replacement for Jack, but in the end he took no action. The PGU concluded that the CPSU's International Department "evidently did not take [the PGU's] warning very seriously and did not insist."

In November 1977, PGU headquarters tried again, sending a memorandum to the Central Committee to complain that the Childs brothers had still not been replaced. The PGU was particularly unhappy that Jack had recently become ill and had been replaced by Morris, who might be under "covert FBI surveillance" because of what the Senate Judiciary Committee had previously written about him. Following up on the memorandum, on November 10 the PGU's Ivanov and Kazakov had another meeting with Gus Hall in Moscow. Hall told the PGU men that he had three candidates in mind to replace Jack, and he elaborated with a complicated plan for how he would let the PGU know which one he had selected. Once again, however, Gus Hall did nothing, and Jack continued his clandestine contacts with the PGU in the United States.

As reported in Operation SOLO, by the spring of 1980 the FBI had become afraid that the Childs brothers were in imminent danger of being compromised. Morris told Hall (the cover story) that unidentified men had been asking his neighbors about him. He was afraid he might have to go into hiding to avoid arrest. He gave Hall whatever CPSU funds he had, then he and Eva retired under FBI protection to a luxury condominium in Florida, where he died on June 2, 1991. Jack, who had been ill for some time, had already died in a New York hospital on August 12, 1980. In effect, the FBI's Operation SOLO ceased to exist after 1980.

We do not believe that in 1980 the Childs brothers were in any danger of being compromised, because we are convinced that the Soviets had known since the 1950s that they were FBI agents. Apart from the PGU's real concerns (as reported in the Mitrokhin Archive), over the years the case shows too many suspicious moments. The brothers always traveled in alias, but when they sometimes used passports given to them by the FBI, the Soviets would have noticed. They certainly would have secretly observed them in their Moscow apartments, where Morris and his wife crawled under the bedclothes with a flashlight to make secret notes for the FBI that Eva tied around her body under her clothes when they left Moscow. On a visit to Moscow in 1964, Jack borrowed an International Department typewriter to send messages "to comrades back home," but he also used it for an encoded letter to an FBI mail drop in New York. In the long run, PGU officers in New York must have observed that whenever the brothers arrived back in the United States, they were swept up by FBI officers to avoid customs and then taken to a special room for immediate debriefing. The New York PGU challenged Jack once when it noticed that he himself had not written down the numbers of the banknotes he had received from the KGB, nor had his wife, as he weakly claimed, because the FBI had done it for him. And so on and so forth. We realize that the FBI was only trying to make things easier for Jack and Morris and that the Childs brothers and their wives were only trying to do a good job for the FBI and the American government. Even so, amateurs should not hope to put one over on yesterday's Soviets or today's Russians.

Finally, we find in Operation SOLO a wonderful explanation for the above altercation between the PGU and Gus Hall. In April 1958, after CPUSA relations with the CPSU were reestablished and Morris went to Moscow for his first meeting with International Department chairman Boris Ponomarev, Ponomarev offered the CPUSA $75,000 for 1958 and $200,000 for 1959 to be sent through the Canadian party for Jack to retrieve. The amount went up and down somewhat, but starting in 1963 it began growing by leaps and bounds, reaching over $1 million in 1967 and over $2 million by 1978, where it remained for most of the 1980s. In 1987, Gus Hall asked for an increase and got over $3 million. When told this, Morris commented only that the Soviets vastly overestimated the influence of the American party.

Instead, we coauthors believe that Gus Hall was being paid off for managing to keep the Childs brothers working for the CPUSA for so many years, in spite of all the PGU's suspicions about them. Because the Soviets knew that Morris and Jack were such trusted FBI agents, they succeeded in using them to persuade the American government—and the world—that the Soviet Union had not been in any way involved with the assassination of President Kennedy and incidentally to turn the focus of lingering investigations toward Cuban émigrés. With Gus Hall's blessing, the Childs brothers had unwittingly made a major contribution to a vitally important Soviet disinformation campaign.

In short, we coauthors are firmly convinced that the leaders of the Soviet Union and of today's Russia were well aware all along that the Childs brothers changed loyalty in the 1950s and became FBI agents. The CPSU not only kept them as agents and close friends, it used them selectively to disseminate false information to the FBI with the knowledge that it would be judged as reliable and passed to the highest levels of the U.S. government.

FIDEL CASTRO JOINS THE PLOT

We now know the real reason why Morris and Jack Childs were treated so royally by the bigwigs of the Soviet Union's Communist Party. Not only were the brothers themselves agreeably gullible, the FBI leadership itself would swallow any disinformation fed to the brothers, vouch for it, and disseminate it to the top leaders of the U.S. government. Not in their wildest dreams could the Soviets have wished for better assets.

We need to keep that in mind when we examine the interesting contacts between Jack Childs and Cuban leader Fidel Castro as masterminded from behind the scenes by the CPSU.

As earlier discussed, it must have been in April 1963, after Lee Harvey Oswald showed the Soviets in Mexico City how he planned to accomplish the assassination of the American president, that the Soviet leadership realized it needed to act. If Oswald couldn't be talked out of it, a very sophisticated disinformation operation would have to be mounted. The most important thing would be to disclaim any Soviet connection with Oswald convincingly, even though he had lived in the Soviet Union for some three years and was known to be an ardent and vocal supporter of Soviet communism and had a Russian wife.

The Soviets evidently decided to turn Oswald into a visible supporter of Cuban communism. When he returned from Mexico in April 1963, Oswald immediately left for New Orleans, where he set himself up as secretary of a Fair Play for Cuba group. For the next few months, he energetically pursued this track, giving speeches to anyone who would listen, talking on the radio, getting into the newspapers, even having fights with

Cuban émigrés. Although Oswald went through the suggested motions, he was clearly not in the least deterred from what he considered his patriotic mission—killing President Kennedy—and then escaping back into the arms of Mother Russia.

Meanwhile, for its part, the KGB disinformation experts were figuring out how Oswald's vehement communism could be slanted toward Cuba instead of the Soviet Union should the unthinkable actually come to pass. Evidently, they suggested that KGB officers in Mexico send Oswald off to New Orleans and to the Fair Play for Cuba charade.

In any case, at some point Fidel Castro was brought into the disinformation planning. Fidel gave quite a performance on November 22 to ensure that the world would know that it had not been he who was behind the assassination and suggested who might have been, and this was naturally in his own self-interest. But Fidel was called upon to assist the Soviet International Department (which had taken on the responsibility for managing Oswald) after the KGB's earlier efforts to deter Oswald from going through with his plan had failed.

The annual international Communist Party meeting was scheduled for May 1963. Normally, Morris Childs would have attended, but he was ill. According to Operation SOLO, the Soviets asked to see Jack Childs, so Gus Hall sent him instead. (We suspect the International Department specifically arranged this with Hall. Morris was perennially unwell, so it would not have been a problem to replace him with Jack.) Jack was very impressed by the reception he got in Moscow: the greetings at the airport, the limousine, the hotel suite, audiences with Suslov and Ponomarev, and dinners with members of the Central Committee and International Department collectively testified to Jack's new status. He was a personal emissary of Hall, the American head of state "temporarily out of power," and therefore above the KGB.

Jack had essentially been serving as a mere bagman for the KGB, and he was a far less complicated man than Morris. That certainly played a role in his contacts with Fidel Castro, and it must also be kept in mind that we learn only Jack's version of these contacts.[22]

Jack was told that Fidel Castro was in Moscow and that all might benefit if they got together. He was warned that Fidel could be mercurial and was told not to tell Fidel anything about Soviet-CPUSA contacts to which the Morrises were privy. The Soviets then arranged for Jack and Fidel, as if by chance, to be seated next to each other at a dinner. They spoke at length in English, ignoring everyone else. Jack was flattered. Fidel said he hoped they would meet again, perhaps in Havana. The Soviet hosts were happy. (Coauthor Pacepa remembers visiting Cuba at about this time in his other life. His main contact there was Raúl Castro, who was the brains of political maneuvers and intelligence operations. Fidel was more the figurehead who followed Raúl's advice. Fidel acted very important, kept people waiting for days to see him, and could rattle on about nothing for hours at a time, but he did as Raúl asked. Here he did as Ponomarev wanted of him.)

In early November 1963, Morris was in Moscow for his annual discussions with the top Soviet leaders about politics and for funding for the CPUSA. Among other things, the Soviets expressed their worries about Fidel Castro, who was supporting revolutionary movements in Latin America haphazardly. Moscow was afraid he didn't know what he was doing and was just self-promoting. The Politburo hoped to use the CPUSA to influence Fidel. International Department chairman Ponomarev observed that Jack and Fidel seemed to hit it off together when they had met in Moscow. They hoped to use this budding relationship for spying on and influencing Fidel, and they confirmed this later.

Ponomarev proposed that Jack travel to Havana under the pretext of delivering a formal message from Gus Hall about cooperation between the communist parties of Cuba and the United States. The Soviets would arrange Jack's travel from Moscow to and from Cuba, so as to avoid U.S. travel restrictions, as well as brief and debrief Jack about his meetings with Fidel.

Jack arrived in Moscow in April 1964. The Soviets stressed that Fidel should be told nothing about their interest in his meeting with Jack. (This was a fishy request since Jack would be flying to and from Moscow in a Soviet airplane. We believe it should be read as a sop to Jack's ego and as deniability in anticipation of Fidel's personal comments on the assassination.)

Jack flew to Havana in mid-May 1964, and as was Fidel's wont, it took him about a week to grant Jack an audience. But when Fidel eventually came over to the villa where Jack was lodging, he was very cordial. They talked about Cuban and American Communist Party relations and setting up better ways to communicate with each other.

Out of the blue, Fidel suddenly asked: "Do you think Oswald killed President Kennedy?" He went on to explain that Oswald could not have done it alone and that there must have been about three people involved. He explained that he and a sharpshooter had tested a rifle like the one Oswald had used, and they concluded that one man could not have done it alone. (This is in accordance with the Soviet disinformation line. Based on Dallas police records, the Warren Commission concluded that on that day, a total of three shots were fired at the president, all from Oswald's Mannlicher-Carcano rifle, from the sixth floor of the School Book Depository, where the three empty shells were found.) Fidel also remarked that, when Oswald was refused a visa at the Cuban embassy in Mexico, he had stormed out saying, "I'm going to kill Kennedy for this." Fidel asked when the Americans were going to catch the other assassins and accepted Jack's suggestion that he write a letter to the American people about it. The discussion then turned to other matters.

Jack left Havana very pleased with himself. He had accomplished all his objectives, establishing a direct link with Fidel Castro for the CPUSA and the hidden link that the Soviets had wanted.

We view all of Jack Childs's contacts with Fidel Castro as having been orchestrated by Boris Ponomarev and one of the many-pronged Soviet disinformation operations designed to reassure the world that the Soviet Union never had anything to do with Lee Harvey Oswald or the assassination of President Kennedy.

CHAPTER 11

THE DESIGNATED HIT MAN

swald was recruited by Soviet foreign intelligence (the PGU) when he
was serving in Japan as a young Marine. What feels hard for people
to swallow, however, is that another PGU department subsequently
trained Oswald as an assassin and so thoroughly brainwashed him that
not even the PGU itself could deter him from accomplishing his very
secret and special "mission for Khrushchev." (For details see Pacepa's
book *Programmed to Kill: Lee Harvey Oswald, the KGB, and Kennedy's
Assassination.*)

Flash back to Oswald's life.[1] Following the example of his two older brothers, as soon as he turned seventeen, Oswald enlisted in the
Marine Corps, eager to escape from the impoverished and chaotic life
imposed on them by their dysfunctional mother. After being trained
in the United States, he arrived in Japan on September 12, 1957, for assignment as a radar operator at Atsugi Air Base (which also had a U-2
reconnaissance plane unit). As a lonely child, Oswald's only pleasure
had been devouring books in the public library, where he had become
hooked on the fairytale descriptions of Marxism and the Soviet Union.
In Japan, unlike his teammates, he showed no interest in sports and
girls, but he did begin going with his teammates to the local bars. There
he spouted off about his favorite subjects, the Soviet paradise and the
Russian language.

It would not have taken the PGU long to recruit a person such as this. At that time Pacepa was urged by his PGU advisors to focus on recruiting an American "serzhant" stationed at Atsugi or Wiesbaden, important Soviet targets for high-altitude radar intelligence. Oswald was soon dating one very expensive bar girl and later seeing another girl for Russian lessons.

In December 1958, Oswald was assigned to El Toro Air Base in California, which did not have U-2s but did have new height-finding radar gear. For security reasons, the PGU did not allow personal meetings with its agents in the United States, but Oswald found ways to go to Tijuana, Mexico, to meet "friends" and also to deposit classified material in bus station lockers that could be retrieved by PGU illegal officers. The Soviets were clearly impressed with his radar information, and Oswald was happy to have found people who appreciated him. Oswald soon developed a determination to spend the rest of his life in the Soviet Union. He managed an early discharge on September 11, 1959, allegedly to care for his sick mother, and on September 20 sailed for Europe on a freighter out of New Orleans. The Soviets did not really want him as a defector, but the PGU arranged to bring him to Moscow "black" for a week in order to debrief him fully on the U-2 flights. It then planned to send him back out as its agent at an international school in Switzerland that it had already arranged for Oswald to contact in March 1959.

Oswald got to Moscow sometime in early October 1959. He was thoroughly debriefed of his information on the U-2. Its most secret attributes were the height at which it flew (thirty thousand meters, or roughly ninety thousand feet) and the new radar used to track it. Oswald was able to provide detailed data on both. Security concerns had caused the U.S. to suspend U-2 flights temporarily, but they were started up again on April 9, 1960, enabling the Soviets to confirm the accuracy of Oswald's reporting. Pacepa learned around this time from PGU chief Aleksandr Sakharovsky that "a defector" had provided the checkable information on the U-2's flight altitude and that the Soviets were ready to shoot down the next flight.

Finally, on May 1, 1960, the Soviets succeeded in bringing down an American U-2 plane. Khrushchev bragged to the world that his rockets had shot it down. In fact, the Soviets did not have rockets able to reach a target at that altitude. If they did, the rocket would have blasted the U-2 and its pilot to smithereens. What the Soviets had actually done was build a special lightweight plane, whose pilot was able to maneuver into the U-2's slipstream and cause it to fall. Thus, both the pilot, Gary Powers, and parts of his U-2 were saved for Khrushchev's exultant show trial and public display.[2]

Khrushchev was riding high, the KGB took all the credit, and Oswald secretly became the hero of the day. Plans to send Oswald to the school in Switzerland were scrapped. At this time, Pacepa heard PGU chief Sakharovsky claim that the downing of the U-2 was "the most valuable May Day present we've ever given the Comrade," meaning Khrushchev.

On November 7, 1960, John F. Kennedy was elected president of the United States, taking office in January 1961. At first Khrushchev merely disdained Kennedy as the spoiled son of a millionaire. But in late January, reliable PGU spies reported that Washington was preparing an assault on Cuba (which would become the Bay of Pigs debacle). Khrushchev exploded with rage. The PGU's Department Thirteen (assassination and sabotage) was called into play. Pacepa recalls that in January 1961, the PGU tasked his Romanian foreign intelligence service to provide the PGU with American English speakers (officers and agents) who could conduct diversion and sabotage operations in the United States. (Up until then, the KGB had trained its officers and agents in British English.)

The hot-headed Khrushchev demanded Kennedy's head. This was how he had always dealt with his enemies. It would not be an easy job for the PGU to pull off in the United States. But in Oswald it already had one devoted and loyal agent who spoke American English and could be trained for the assignment. Oswald was told that his idol Khrushchev had specially asked for him to be sent temporarily to the United States on a very secret mission, after which he would of course return home to the Soviet Union. Flattered, Oswald could not refuse.

Then things started to heat up. The U.S. embassy in Moscow received an undated letter from Oswald in Minsk on February 13, 1961, in which he stated that he wanted to return to the United States. On April 17, the Bay of Pigs fiasco took place. The PGU immediately ordered its satellite services, including Pacepa's in Romania, to "throw mud" on "the Pig," Khrushchev's new name for President Kennedy. On May 25 Oswald wrote the U.S. embassy in Moscow that he had gotten married and wanted to take his Russian wife with him to the U.S. Pacepa's PGU advisors always insisted that every illegal officer or agent have a trained wife to help him with communications and to bolster his morale. On June 2 and 3, Khrushchev met Kennedy in Vienna—a meeting that reinforced his hatred for him. Just after that event, coauthor Pacepa saw a letter Khrushchev had sent to Ceausescu and probably to the other satellite leaders calling Kennedy a puppet of the CIA and the American military-industrial complex. Khrushchev stepped up tension over Berlin, and on August 13, the Berlin Wall was built overnight.

After persuading him to return to the U.S. on a very secret, temporary mission, Department Thirteen would have put Oswald through some intensive training as he was not a trained agent. Our best guide to his training would be the example of "Anton," a case very similar to Oswald's. Born in Canada, "Anton" returned with his family to his fanatical communist father's native Czechoslovakia at the age of sixteen. There "Anton" was recruited by the Czech secret police and in 1957 was turned over to the Soviet PGU's Department Thirteen for assassinations abroad and sent to Moscow for training. His assignment was to return to Canada to perform "special tasks," which would be specified after he was settled in Canada.

In 1958 "Anton" entered training near Moscow, where he was comfortably lodged in a safe house, by officers of Department Thirteen. Pacepa's Romanian DIE also had its own such division, known as Group Z—the last letter of the alphabet, standing for the final solution—which similarly had its own training facilities. "Anton's" instruction focused on all kinds of clandestine communications: ciphers, codes, invisible writing, microdots, recognition signals, and radio procedures.

In 1962, Oswald worked for a short time at a graphic arts company in Dallas, where he discussed the making of microdots with another employee. He also used the company's equipment to make identity documents for himself under the alias O. H. Lee, which he used for travel to Mexico, in fake documents certifying his vaccinations, and to receive weapons at post office boxes, including the rifle that would kill Kennedy.

"Anton" also became an excellent marksman by practicing at a special firing range on targets depicting a man's upper body.

When Oswald was arrested after the assassination, he still had in his proud possession a hunting license issued to him in Minsk, a membership certificate in the Belorussian Society of Hunters and Fishermen, and a gun permit, all issued in the summer of 1960.

"Anton" had studied the vulnerabilities of sabotage targets and on the side had endured a little academic instruction in Marxism.

Oswald did not need sabotage instruction, as he knew what his assignment was, but he undoubtedly had plenty of morale-building brainwashing sessions.

Unlike Oswald, "Anton" never knew what his exact assignment would be, although he was told that "if a need for a weapon develops, one will be provided." After "Anton" completed his training, his principal Department Thirteen training officer was assigned to the United Nations in New York so as to be available to "Anton," but for the time being "Anton" simply remained in Canada awaiting further instructions. In 1972 "Anton" was arrested by Canadian authorities, with whom he then fully cooperated.[3]

In Moscow, it took over a year for the U.S. embassy, on May 24, 1962, to issue proper papers for the Oswalds (now including daughter June, born February 15, 1962) to travel to the U.S. On June 1, 1962, the family finally left the Soviet Union on their long trip to Fort Worth, Texas, where Oswald's brother Robert took them in.

Materials found after Oswald's death indicate that he knew Department Thirteen officer Valery Kostikov by the operational pseudonym "Comrade Kostin" before meeting him in Mexico City in 1963. It is very likely that Kostikov participated in Oswald's training in the Moscow area and then went to Mexico City, just as "Anton's" training officer from Moscow was assigned to the United Nations in New York when "Anton" repatriated to Canada. Kostikov was assigned as a Soviet diplomat to Mexico City in September 1961 shortly before Oswald's anticipated repatriation to the United States.

PGU illegal officer George de Mohrenschildt moved back to the Dallas area in October 1961, evidently in order to help the Oswalds settle down there at that time. Oswald's departure from the Soviet Union was delayed simply as the result of bureaucracy at the U.S. embassy in Moscow in getting its paperwork to the Oswalds.

A SECRET PROMISE TO KHRUSHCHEV

It is hard for normal citizens to understand what it was like to be Oswald, enthralled, some would say brainwashed, by the Soviets. The whole focus of his life during his "temporary" return to the United States was to carry out the very secret mission that Khrushchev had personally entrusted to him—to kill President Kennedy, who had destroyed Khrushchev's international prestige. Then Oswald could return to his own life with his beloved new family in the Soviet paradise.[4]

We do not know if Khrushchev ever spoke to Oswald in person, but he very well might have. We do know that Khrushchev personally decorated Bogdan Stashinsky for having killed two prominent Soviet émigrés living in West Germany. Oswald did Khrushchev a huge favor in 1960 in enabling the Soviets to bring down Gary Powers and his U-2 spy plane. So during his training for the mission in the United States, Oswald was certainly told that Khrushchev had personally asked him to perform a top secret assassination for him. Marina, Oswald's wife, would tell her biographer that her husband had once complained that Kennedy's "papa bought him the presidency," an echo of Khrushchev's oft-repeated disdain for Kennedy as "the millionaire's kid." Yet nothing indicates that Oswald himself had ever developed any personal animus against Kennedy.

Soon after the Oswalds' arrival in Texas in 1962, they sought out other Russian émigrés. According to one young man who used to visit the Oswalds to practice his Russian, Lee described Khrushchev as "simply brilliant." He also liked President Kennedy; on their living room table, the Oswalds "more or less permanently" displayed a copy of *Life* magazine with a photo of Kennedy on the cover. Marina Oswald would testify to the Warren Commission in 1964 that her husband had once said: "If someone had killed Hitler in time, it would have saved many lives." That could well have been the theme-song of Oswald's Department Thirteen training.

Shortly before the Oswalds left the Soviet Union, the pregnant Marina visited "two aunts in Kharkov" for three or four weeks. This was undoubtedly time spent with Department Thirteen officers, who trained her how best to support her husband physically and emotionally and in clandestine communications. Marina was not, however, told what her husband's secret mission was. Oswald understood the extreme secrecy of his mission, and he was also very protective of his wife and did not want her to suffer from sharing his life. Upon arriving in Texas in 1962, Oswald told his mother: "Not even Marina knows why I have returned to the United States." He also did not want his wife to hang out with Russian-American women, going shopping, or practicing speaking English, because he was determined to see his family return to live out the rest of their lives in the

Soviet paradise, where she would have no need for American products or the English language. Neither did he want Marina's life complicated by his own frequent changes of residence, so he was happy when she became friends with the kindly American Ruth Paine over Russian lessons and began staying with her as Oswald became preoccupied with his mission. Starting on February 17, 1963, he had Marina write to the Soviet embassy in Washington, DC, to say that she wanted to return to the Soviet Union. She wrote again with the same request on March 17. On July 1 Oswald himself wrote to the embassy, asking for separate visas, with a plea to rush Marina's so that she could give birth to her second child in the Soviet motherland. Then Marina herself wrote again on July 8. The embassy fudged in every case, saying it had to check with Moscow or asking for more documents.

The only other person who was close to Oswald after his return to the United States was the supposedly wealthy and aristocratic Russian émigré George de Mohrenschildt. He became Oswald's best friend and mentor, but no one could ever really explain how they had come to know each other. Actually, de Mohrenschildt was an old, experienced KGB illegal officer who had become an American citizen and whose main job since at least 1938 had been to collect military intelligence.

On December 22, 1958, Oswald was assigned to El Toro Base in Texas. That was most likely when the KGB first assigned de Mohrenschildt to guide the inexperienced, nineteen-year-old Oswald both in the everyday logistics of being an agent and in the kind of intelligence Moscow needed. De Mohrenschildt's role in Oswald's story is fascinating, but it is clear that in 1962 he did not know why Oswald had returned to the United States.

Let us look briefly at the illegal officer George de Mohrenschildt himself. Allegedly born in 1911, he was handsome, charming, changed his background story many times during his lifetime, had many love affairs, and was married four times. His last wife, Jeanne, was also an illegal officer and had been publicly denounced as a communist spy by a previous husband. George first came to the United States in 1938 on a Polish passport documenting him as Baron George von Mohrenschildt, the son of a German director of the Swedish "Nobel interests" in the Baku oilfields. His intelligence assignment was to mix with conservative German-Americans and try to pick up Nazi military information. When it became clear that the Nazis were losing the war, he became the French

George de Mohrenschildt, who had attended a commercial school in Belgium founded by Napoleon. After the war he claimed his father had been a Russian engineer working in the Ploesti oilfields in Romania who was captured and executed by the Soviet army. In whatever guise, de Mohrenschildt's job was to collect military intelligence.

De Mohrenschildt was most likely the PGU illegal officer who collected Oswald's information on U.S. Air Force planes from bus station lockers in the U.S. and at personal meetings in Tijuana when Oswald was assigned to El Toro Base in Texas. As an American citizen, de Mohrenschildt could freely move around in the United States. He and his wife, Jeanne, are known to have been in Mexico at the time of Oswald's meetings with "friends" in Tijuana. Oswald wasn't yet twenty years old when he decided he wanted to defect to the Soviet Union. For all his bravado, until then he'd been moved around on instructions from his peripatetic mother or the U.S. Marine Corps, so he badly needed advice from the older and more experienced de Mohrenschildt. When Oswald was discharged from the Marines on September 11, 1959, he immediately went to New Orleans, booked passage for Le Havre on an unlisted freighter of the Lykes Lines, and sailed for Le Havre the next day, September 20. (On his own, the inexperienced Oswald would not have known about the Lykes Line freighter that took him to Europe, but it was an inconspicuous and inexpensive line often used by de Mohrenschildt.)

When Oswald returned to the United States in 1962, his contacts with Russian-Americans in the Dallas area provided a pretext for how he might have met de Mohrenschildt. But every time either of them was asked about it, the story changed. De Mohrenschildt kindly helped the Oswalds get settled and resettled, but he mistakenly assumed that Oswald's KGB job was more or less the same as his own had been, i.e., to collect military intelligence, as Oswald had done when he was in the Marines. Upon Oswald's return to the United States, de Mohrenschildt went to a lot of trouble to find ways to introduce him to interesting military people but then was completely baffled when Oswald made no effort to follow up on any of those attractive leads. Clearly, not even de Mohrenschildt, Oswald's "best friend" and mentor and PGU advisor, knew the real reason Oswald had come back to the United States.

Only Oswald knew what Khrushchev wanted him to do, and although Oswald was only twenty-three years old, he was determined to accomplish his secret mission for his idol Khrushchev and, at all costs, to keep it entirely secret.

The Soviet embassy in Washington was not involved in Oswald's return to the United States. The PGU station there was responsible for keeping track of the Oswalds' whereabouts in the United States, for replying to the Oswalds' letters—which it did coldly—and finally for preventing their return to the Soviet Union, just as Moscow had instructed it to do. That was surely all until further instruction if the inconceivable (or the inevitable) occurred.

Department Thirteen had assigned its officer Valery Kostikov to Mexico City in September 1961 to provide Oswald with moral support and operational advice. After his unsuccessful trip to Mexico City in April 1963, Oswald understood that he would have to rely on his own wits to accomplish his mission, but he still needed official assistance to return legally and safely to the Soviet motherland. When the Soviet embassy in Washington kept giving him and his wife the runaround about getting visas for the Soviet Union, he decided to try getting visas in Mexico for Moscow via Havana. After unsuccessfully seeking to visit his case officer Kostikov in Mexico City again in September–October 1963, and with unfriendly officials at the Cuban embassy, he gave up and retreated to Texas, hoping to be able to work out an escape mechanism by himself when the time came.

Oswald's working draft of a letter dated November 9, 1963, addressed to the Soviet embassy in Washington was found after the assassination at Ruth Paine's house, where Oswald had gone to join his wife and children after his second fruitless visit to Mexico. In it, he explains that he talked to "Comrade Kostine" at the Soviet embassy in Mexico City but that the embassy was unprepared and couldn't help him with the visas he and his family needed, stressing that the Soviet embassy was not to blame but was simply unprepared for him. He complains, however, that the Cuban consulate was "guilty of a gross breach of regulations." Once again he asks for the entrance visas "as soon as they come" while informing the embassy of the birth of his second daughter on October 20, 1963.

Oswald tried hard to be polite with Soviet officialdom, but by this time he must have understood that no help would be forthcoming from them. Left hanging high and dry, he was still convinced that he alone understood what Khrushchev wanted him to do. He had made a solemn promise to the Soviet leader, and he was going to fulfill that promise even if none of the stupid KGB bureaucrats would cooperate. Taking matters into his own hands, Oswald shot and killed President Kennedy on November 22, 1963.

Fidel Castro was already prepared to do his part, so two days later, Cuban agent Jack Ruby shot and killed Oswald at the Dallas Police station. On October 5, 1966, Ruby's death sentence was overturned and a new trial ordered. That December, Ruby was diagnosed with acute lung cancer, and he died on January 3, 1967.

The Russians have used radioactive weapons to kill their enemies in the West often. On July 22, 1978, Romanian leader Nicolae Ceausescu ordered Pacepa to have a Romanian émigré in the West, Noel Bernard, killed. Bernard directed the Romanian program at Radio Free Europe in Munich, whose broadcasts constantly attacked the Romanian dictator. Bernard was to be administered a lethal radioactive substance the Romanians had gotten from the Soviets. Instead, Pacepa defected the next day and sent a warning to Bernard. Bernard insisted on continuing with his job. On December 23, 1981, three years after Pacepa was granted political asylum in the U.S., Noel Bernard died of a galloping form of cancer later confirmed as the result of a radioactive poison administered by Romanian foreign intelligence.

George de Mohrenschildt and his wife stayed in Haiti until 1967, when they quietly sailed for the U.S. with their household effects and some $250,000 from a mysterious deposit that had been made to his Haitian bank account. The Warren Commission had already absolved de Mohrenschildt of any connection with the JFK assassination. Pacepa knew in Romania that George de Mohrenschildt was a KGB asset but nothing more about him or his activities. On March 29, 1977, de Mohrenschildt was interviewed by the writer Edward Jay Epstein about Oswald at the Breakers Hotel in Palm Beach. There de Mohrenschildt learned from Epstein that the House Select Commission on Assassinations was scheduled to interview him. At the lunch break, de Mohrenschildt went to his daughter's home in nearby Manalapan (where he was staying) and shot himself in the head.

De Mohrenschildt's widow provided some materials he had left behind, including a manuscript in which the alleged German baron praised Khrushchev: "He is gone now, God bless his Bible-quoting soul and his earthy personality. His sudden bursts of anger and beating of the table with his shoe, are all gone and belong to history. Millions of Russians miss him."[5] The manuscript also described Oswald as a nervous marksman who admired Kennedy and could not have killed him. It suggested that President Lyndon Johnson was behind the assassination because he hated the whole Kennedy clan. In other words, de Mohrenschildt was doing his best to support the post-assassination disinformation narratives.

The House Commission concluded its investigation without accusing anyone of conspiring with Oswald in the Kennedy assassination. The CIA was specifically absolved of any responsibility.

In the end, there is no doubt that Lee Harvey Oswald was trained by the KGB's Department Thirteen to commit the assassination of President John F. Kennedy, as ordered by Nikita Khrushchev. Even after the Russian political scene had changed and the KGB ordered Oswald to stand down, Oswald stubbornly went ahead with what he considered his personal mission as bestowed upon him by his hero, Khrushchev.

Ultimately, the Russian government must bear the responsibility for President Kennedy's death.

THE COVER-UP: A DISINFORMATION EMPIRE IN THE WEST

"Dezinformatsiya works like cocaine," KGB chief Yuri Andropov preached in his days at the Lubyanka. "If you sniff it once or twice, it may not change your life. Use it day after day, though, it will make you into an addict, a different man." During the Cold War, non-communist Western information outlets willing to publish the KGB's fabricated stories without sourcing them were hard to find. To solve that problem, the KGB created its own organizations and masqueraded them as Western. Persuading the rest of the world that the Soviet Union had nothing to do with Kennedy's assassination became one of the most important tasks of its secret intelligence service's vast disinformation machinery that eventually commanded more undercover intelligence officers than the rest of the KGB had.

The first Russian international disinformation organization was founded under the respectable name of the World Peace Council. At first its main function was to document that America was a war-mongering, Zionist country financed by Jews and their money, run by a rapacious "Council of the Elders of Zion" (a derisive epithet for the U.S. Congress, a "Trilateral Commission," or other secretive cronyist society), the aim of which was to convert the globe into a Jewish fiefdom. This material was all concocted by the Soviet foreign intelligence service.

To make the World Peace Council seem to be an indigenous Western organization, the Kremlin headquartered it in Paris and persuaded the leftist French Nobel prizewinner Frédéric Joliot-Curie to chair it. Back in those days, however, the French government saw through the ruse, accused the World Peace Council of being a Russian *dezinformatsiya* front, and kicked it out of France. One of Russia's most trusted influence agents of that period, French philosopher Jean-Paul Sartre, tried to persuade the French government to recant its decision. Sartre publicly vilified the United States as a racist nation suffering from political rabies,[6] but that didn't do the trick. A few months later, the World Peace Council was moved to Soviet-occupied Vienna.

It is no wonder the WPC was expelled from France. Behind its supposedly French façade, the WPC was as purely Soviet as it gets. Its daily business was conducted by a Soviet-style secretariat, whose twenty-one members were undercover intelligence officers from seven Soviet bloc countries (USSR, Poland, Czechoslovakia, Bulgaria, Hungary, Romania, and East Germany). The WPC also had twenty-three vice presidents, all undercover intelligence officers or agents. Four represented Soviet bloc countries (USSR, Poland, East Germany, and Romania), three represented communist governments loyal to Moscow (North Korea, North Vietnam, and Angola), one represented the African National Congress—which was financed and manipulated by Moscow—four represented non-ruling communist parties (in the United States, France, Italy, and Argentina), and eleven represented national-level WPC affiliates in the Soviet bloc and other Soviet puppet countries.

Most of the WPC's permanent employees were undercover Soviet bloc intelligence officers trained in "peace operations" whose true role was to shape the new Western peace movements into fifth columns for the socialist camp. The WPC's two publications in French, *Nouvelles perspectives* and *Courier de la Paix*, were also managed by undercover Soviet intelligence and Romanian DIE[7] officers.

The money for the WPC budget came largely from Moscow, delivered by Soviet intelligence in the form of laundered cash dollars to hide its origin. In 1989, when the Soviet Union was on the verge of collapse, the WPC publicly admitted that 90 percent of its money came from the KGB.[8]

When the Soviet army was withdrawn from Austria, WPC headquarters was moved to Prague.

During the Vietnam War, the Russians tried to make the WPC look "nonaligned" by moving its headquarters to Helsinki. In those days, the Soviet bloc operated with a virtually free hand in Finland, because President Urho Kaleva Kekkonen was a highly regarded KGB agent. According to KGB defector Oleg Gordievsky, Kekkonen had been fruitfully manipulated by the KGB until 1981, at which time he ended his unprecedented twenty-five-year term as president of Finland. During most of those years, his case officer was Viktor Vladimirov, a onetime chief of the KGB station in Helsinki. Vladimirov was promoted to the rank of KGB general for his successful handling of Kekkonen.[9]

To give more credibility to the WPC's alleged "nonaligned" appearance, Moscow also appointed an "apolitical" Indian, Romesh Chandra, as its chairman. In reality, Chandra was a Soviet intelligence agent infiltrated into the National Committee of the Communist Party of India, one of the foreign communist parties most loyal to the Soviet Union at that time.[10]

After the Soviet Union collapsed, the World Peace Council moved to Athens, but its honorary chairman was still Romesh Chandra. In the 1970s the WPC required all its branches to initiate demonstrations around the world to protest America's Zionist government and its militaristic sharks.

Over the years, the KGB created similar disinformation organizations in every part of Western society. Here are just a few in which Gen. Pacepa was directly involved: the World Federation of Democratic Youth, headquartered in Budapest, which had 210 national affiliates and published *Jeunesse mondiale* and *Nouvelles de la FMDJ*; the International Union of Students, headquartered in Prague, which had eighty national student organizations and published *Nouvelles du monde étudiant*; the World Federation of Trade Unions, headquartered in Prague, which was joined by ninety national organizations and published *Le movement sindicale mondial* and *Trade Union Flashes*; and the International Federation of Democratic Women, headquartered in East Berlin, which had branches in the Middle East, Africa, Asia, and South America, was joined by 129 national organizations, and published *Women in the World* in eight foreign languages.

Until President Kennedy's assassination, the tasks of these huge machineries were to change Europe's old hatred for the Nazis into one for

Zionist America, the new occupation power. In other words, to try once again to exploit latent antisemitism to scare Europe and the Islamic world into thinking America intended to transform them into Jewish fiefdoms.

After President Kennedy's assassination, these disinformation organizations spent most of their efforts trying to persuade the world that the United States had murdered its own president in a coup plot. Most Western European leftists, who had never set foot in America, were game to regarding far-away America with contempt just as these disinformation organizations painted it to them. That is, as a Zionist realm financed by Jewish money and run by a rapacious "Council of the Elders of Zion," whose intelligence services assassinated its domestic enemies, even its own president.

To get that image across, these international disinformation organizations portrayed everyone and everything in America as subordinated to Jewish interests: the leaders, the government, the political parties, the most prominent personalities—even American history. Their goal was to make people in Europe "feel sick to their stomachs just thinking about America." It would appear that they succeeded. During Pacepa's last years in Romania, millions of Western Europeans took to the streets, not to celebrate the freedoms they enjoyed because America had liberated them from under the Nazi boot and protected them from that of the Soviets but to condemn America's war-mongering Zionist government.

In the early 1970s, KGB chairman Yuri Andropov, the father of Russia's modern era of deceit, decided to turn the Islamic world into an explosive enemy of the United States. Islam and the Arab world, General Sakharovsky had preached, were petri dishes in which his disinformation machinery could nurture a virulent strain of America-hate from the bacterium of Marxist-Leninist thought. Islam's doctrine of soul-purifying jihad was the twin to our own soul-purifying romance with revolutionary nihilism. The Muslims' anti-Semitism ran deep. We had only to keep repeating our themes: that the United States was a "Zionist country bankrolled by rich Jews, who wanted to transform the rest of the world into a Jewish fiefdom."

As Sakharovsky described it, Islam was obsessed with preventing the infidel's occupation of its territory. It would be highly receptive to the dogma that American Zionism was the source of all evil. Muslims would instantly applaud our characterization of the U.S. Congress as a rapacious

Zionist body aiming to turn the world into a Jewish fiefdom. That would redirect the historic Arab and Islamic hostility, nationalism, and vulgar anti-Semitism to focus on the United States. Fervent anti-Americanism would spread just the way Sakharovsky had planned. September 11, 2001 and September 11, 2012 are heartrending proof of that.

CHAPTER 12

FROM PRESIDENTIAL ASSASSINATION TO INTERNATIONAL TERRORISM

History usually repeats itself. If you have lived two lives, as Gen. Pacepa has done, you have a good chance of seeing that reenactment with your own eyes. The Kremlin's cover-up of President Kennedy's assassination vividly recalls the cover-up of the 1973 assassination of Cleo A. Noel Jr., the U.S. ambassador to Sudan. At that time, Pacepa was still an adviser to the president of Romania and deputy head of that country's espionage service. Here is the insider's view of what really went on then. There are lessons to be learned here not only about the handling of the JFK assassination but about the conduct of today's international terrorism.

In 1973, PLO leader Yasser Arafat's liaison officer for Romania, Hani al-Hassan (nom de guerre Abu Hasan), let his Romanian contact know that Arafat had sent a commando unit to Sudan headed by his top deputy, Abu Jihad (née Khalil al-Wazir), to carry out an operation codenamed "Nahr al-Barad" (Cold River) as payback for the destruction of a Palestinian training camp by Israeli fighter jets eleven days earlier. Abu Jihad's task was to take a few American diplomats in Khartoum hostage whom Arafat wanted to use as bargaining chips to "free" Sirhan Sirhan, the Palestinian assassin of Robert Kennedy.

"Stop him!" Ceausescu yelled when Pacepa told him the news. Ceausescu knew that Arafat had been trained in terrorism at the KGB's Balashikha special-operations school,[1] and he now feared that, due to his close

169

relationship with Arafat, his carefully cultivated world image that he was independent of Moscow might be compromised.

It was too late. After President Nixon refused the terrorists' demand, the PLO commando unit executed three of their hostages: U.S. ambassador Cleo A. Noel Jr.; his deputy, George Curtis Moore; and Belgian chargé d'affaires Guy Eid.

In 1978, Pacepa was granted political asylum in the U.S. Soon after, a former analyst for the National Security Agency (NSA) provided Pacepa solid evidence that Arafat himself had ordered those murders. He also gave Pacepa the transcripts of the secretly recorded radio communications between Arafat and Abu Jihad in the operation. According to these documents, on March 2, 1973, at around 8:00 p.m. local time, Arafat radioed the order to execute the hostages. Because an hour later the international media had still not reported the killing, Arafat reiterated, via his Racal radio the order to kill the hostages. Later that same day, Arafat radioed his gunmen again, telling them to release Saudi and Jordanian diplomats and to surrender themselves to Sudanese authorities. "Explain your just cause to [the] great Sudanese Arab masses and international opinion. We are with you on the same road."

The U.S. government never charged Arafat with this crime in a court of law or even in the court of public opinion. Hence Arafat, who played a major role in creating today's international terrorism, was granted the Nobel Prize for peace in 1994. Four years later, Arafat was received with grand honors at the White House, where President Bill Clinton highly praised him.[2]

The 2012 terrorist attack in Benghazi that murdered Ambassador J. Christopher Stevens and three of his subordinates on September 11, 2012, was the assassination of U.S. Ambassador Noel revisited. Both had been carried out by Muslims armed with Soviet-made rocket-propelled grenades, Kalashnikovs, and Molotov cocktails; both organizers were known; and both remained unpunished. After days of secret deliberation, the Obama administration claimed to have discovered the "real" culprit: *Innocence of Muslims*, an obscure documentary movie made by an unknown Israeli-American director, Nakoula Basseley Nakoula (aka Sam Bacile). The U.S. administration officially informed the world that the murders in Benghazi and the assault on U.S. embassies all over the Middle East were simply "spontaneous" reactions to the film. Case closed. Just as Arafat's murder of ambassador Noel is still closed.

To make this conclusion credible, no result of the autopsy on Stevens's body was released. According to the Arabic media, he "was sexually raped before being killed by the gunmen who stormed the embassy's building in Benghazi."[3] Ambassador Stevens was quietly buried in his native town. Not with national honors at Arlington Cemetery, as Ambassador Noel was.

It is even more noteworthy that no representative of the Obama administration attended the October 2012 ceremony honoring Ambassador Stevens's heroism. The highest officials present were former U.S. Secretary of State George P. Schultz, former Undersecretary of State Thomas R. Pickering, and the Libyan ambassador to the U.S.[4]

One can only hope that President Trump's administration will expose the truth about both assassinations and establish measures to protect the United States from other similar terrorist attacks.

CHAPTER 13

THE KING IS DEAD! LONG LIVE THE KING!

On February 22, 1939, the world learned that the Soviet Union was secretly planning to take over the world with the help of devastating bacteriological and chemical weapons. Encouraged by the pact with Hitler, the Soviets' Marshal Kliment Voroshilov—who would later succeed Stalin for a few months—publicly stated: "Ten years ago or more the Soviet Union signed a convention abolishing the use of poison gas and bacteriological warfare.[1] To that we still adhere, but if our enemies use such methods against us, I tell you that we *are* prepared—fully prepared—to use them against aggressors on their own soil."[2] The government of the Soviet Union did indeed sign the 1925 Geneva Biological Weapons Convention, updated in December 2017, which prohibited the research and production of bacteriological weapons, but it never respected it.

"In today's world, where nuclear arms have made military wars obsolete, our main weapon should be terrorism." That was what the KGB General Sakharovsky used to preach twenty years later, when he was the intelligence adviser to communist Romania. According to him, just several tons of *Novichok*, a Russian nerve agent—at that time still under development—would have been enough to kill all human life in the non-communist world. (In 2018, a Russian military defector, Sergei Skripal, and his daughter were poisoned in England by Russian intelligence with a diluted form of *Novichok*, but the British, now familiar with this poison weapon, were able to save their lives.)

In 1989 Soviet communism collapsed, but the new "democratic" Russia was still mass producing bacteriological weapons. We learned that from Vladimir Pasechnik, the first major defector from the super-secret Russian biological warfare program, who in 1989 was granted political asylum in the United Kingdom. Pasechnik alerted Western intelligence to a super-secret Soviet biological warfare (BW) program, known as *Biopreparat*, and cowrote a book on this subject entitled *Liquid Crystals*. According to Pasechnik's revelations, the *Biopreparat* program was ten times larger than the Western intelligence community had suspected. Pasechnik died of a stroke in 1993. According to his son Nikita, Pasechnik expected to be killed by the KGB—or later by its successor, the FSB—because of his disclosures.

In 1992, Col. Kanatzhan Alibekov, the number-two scientist of Russia's super-secret biological weapons program, defected to the United States. According to his revelations, partially published by the National Defense University Press in 2016, the first major Soviet biological weapons systems were secretly developed in a laboratory hidden in Moscow and headed by Yakov M. Fishman until 1937, when he was assassinated during Stalin's Great Purge, in order to preserve the secrecy of his work.[3]

Also in 1992, Russia's first freely elected president, Boris Yeltsin, publicly admitted that his country was operating an offensive bioweapons program in violation of the Biological Weapons Convention that Russia had signed. Yeltsin's admission was temporary, rejected by his successor, President Vladimir Putin. "What is the future preparing for us?" he rhetorically asked in a 2012 interview with the Moscow *Rosiiskaya Gazeta*. "In the more distant future, weapon systems based on new principles (beam, geophysical, wave, genetic, psychophysical, and other technologies) will be developed. All these will, in addition to nuclear weapons, provide entirely new instruments for achieving our political and strategic goals. Such high-tech weapons systems will be comparable in effect to nuclear weapons, but they will be more 'acceptable' in terms of political and military ideology."[4]

To the best of our knowledge, today's Russia still has its highly secret Biopreparat program, which is now involved in producing the new and more devastating generation of bioweapons suggested by President Putin. The Biopreparat facilities are still among the most secret secrets of that country, but in real life few secrets remain secret forever. The

Russian media of these days has already revealed that the reorganized Biopreparat program has eighteen labs, production centers, and test sites. Among them are the Kirov bioweapons production facility, the Zagorsk smallpox production facility, the Berdsk bioweapons production facility, the Sverdlovsk weaponized anthrax center, and the Aralsk-7 biological weapons test site.[5]

So far, we do not have hard proof attesting that Russia has given communist China the technology for producing the novel coronavirus. An accident at Russia's Arask-7 ultra-secret test site, however, did reveal that Russia secretly weaponized several biological weapons quite similar to the coronavirus: *B. anthracis, F. tulaenis, Y. pestis, Coxiella burnetiid,* and *Brucela suis.*

Soon after the Soviet bloc collapsed, researchers at Germany's Max Planck Institute for Human Cognitive and Brain Sciences in the now liberated Leipzig discovered a genetic factor, the A1 mutation, which affects the ability to learn from past mistakes. On April 12, 2003, thousands of Americans, presumably infected by the A1 mutation, began sermonizing that capitalism was America's real enemy and that it should be replaced with socialism by redistributing the country's wealth. Quite a few young Americans cheered. They were, of course, galvanized by the prospect that a Democratic administration would force rich Americans to pay for young people's own health care, mortgages, loans, and school tuition.

In September 2007, tens of thousands of young Americans attended an anticapitalist meeting in San Francisco, and on March 20, 2010, many more took to the streets in Washington, D.C., in a chain of so-called spontaneous demonstrations. In reality, these events were organized by a Moscow-financed outfit, A.N.S.W.E.R (Act Now to Stop War and End Racism), which had sloshed out of the Workers World Party (WWP), a KGB front when Gen. Pacepa was at the top of its community. In typical Soviet style, A.N.S.W.E.R generously supplied buses to transport the "spontaneous" demonstrators and posted ready-to-use flyers on its website to be downloaded, printed, and passed around. At that time, A.N.S.W.E.R had large headquarters in ten major U.S. cities.

In November 2008, over 60 million Americans, most of whom had no longer been taught real history in schools, became galvanized by a socialist pledge to redistribute the country's wealth in order to "change" the "rotting" America, and they gave their votes to the Party of Change. Soon, the United States was changed from a country belonging to "We the People" into one managed by a kind of a socialist *nomenklatura* with unchecked power, like the socialist Romanian *nomenklatura* to which Pacepa once belonged.

"We have to pass the bill so that you can find out what is in it," the leader of the U.S. House of Representatives *nomenklatura* once told the media.[6] That was a first in U.S. history. It did not take long before this American *nomenklatura* started to take control of banks, home mortgages, school loans, automakers, and most of the health care industry. When tens of thousands of Americans disagreed with this transfer of wealth from private hands to the government, the Congressional *nomenklatura* called them Nazis. That was also what Ceausescu's *nomenklatura* had called its critics.

God forbid comparing the United States with the bankrupt socialist Romania of those days, but we believe there is a dramatic lesson behind this figure of speech. On August 15, 1947, the Politburo of Romania's Communist Party, which had just taken over the country's helm, converted Romania's old currency, called the *leu* (lion), into a new *socialist leu*. Each Romanian, regardless of how much money he owned, received the same small amount of the new currency. From one day to the next, there were no more Romanians owning more than the equivalent of a couple hundred dollars. In other words, there were no longer capitalists in Romania. A few months later, private properties were nationalized, and on December 30, 1947, Romania was officially declared a socialist country.

In 1948, when the Romanian socialist *nomenklatura* nationalized the oil industry, that country was the second-greatest oil exporter in Europe. Thirty years later, Romania was a heavy importer of oil, gasoline was rationed, the temperature in public places had to be kept under 63 degrees, and all shops had to close no later than 5:30 p.m. to save energy.

Once the second-largest oil and grain exporter in Europe, Romania was starving in those days. One of the most astonishing failures of Russian-style socialism was also the regularity with which its political triumphs produced economic ruin. Whether in transforming that country from the world's greatest grain exporter at the time of the 1917 revolution into the world's greatest grain importer, or in devastating Ethiopia's economy to the point that its famine stirred the compassion of the entire world, Russian-style socialism invariably destroyed the national economy wherever it came to power.

In 2011, the new "democratic" Russia unleashed another weapon of mass destruction: anti-Americanism. On October 6, 2011, in a broadcast in English, a pro-Russian Cuban radio station that calls itself "A Friendly Voice Around the World" announced that the Workers World Party (a Marxist organization financed by Moscow) had decided to join the Occupy Wall Street demonstrations "against the capitalist system and in favor of a socialist future." Radio Havana also reported that a Workers World Party conference to be held on October 8 and 9 in the Bronx in New York City would debate, "from a Marxist perspective," America's current "economic crisis." "Long live the revolution! Long live socialism!" Others in Chicago and Philadelphia marched with communist flags. In L.A., a speaker advocated violence, as in the French revolution, which "made fundamental transformations, but it was bloody." He supported bloody revolution in the U.S., too, because "Ultimately, the bourgeoisie won't go without violent means...Long live revolution. Long live socialism." Marxism is on the march again, and it has not even bothered to change its old clothes. Others in Chicago and Philadelphia marched with communist flags.

Anti-Semitism has raised its head too. "I think the Zionist Jews who are running these banks and our Federal Reserve...need to be run out of this country," declared one Los Angeles occupier. "Jewish money controls American politics," a New York occupier complained. Still others yelled that "Jews control Wall Street."[7] These are the identical slogans spread by Gen. Pacepa's DIE around the world during the Cold War, when Moscow went out of its way to portray the United States as an "imperial Zionist country" financed by Jewish money and run by a rapacious "Council of the Elders of Zion" (the KGB's favorite epithet for the U.S. Congress) in order to transform the world into a Jewish fiefdom.

On November 7, 2017, the new "democratic" Russia celebrated one hundred years since armed Bolsheviks had installed communism in Russia. For the rest of the world, however, that day marked the beginning of one of the worst mass-killing eras in history. According to a recent estimate by the prestigious Hudson Institute, "the victims include 200,000 killed during the Red Terror (1918–22); 11 million dead from famine and dekulakization; 700,000 executed during the Great Terror (1937–38);

400,000 more executed between 1929 and 1953; 1.6 million dead during forced population transfers; and a minimum 2.7 million dead in the gulags, labor colonies and special settlements.[8]

Now a new generation of Americans want to transform the United States into a Russian-style country. According to an August 5, 2012, article published in the *New York Times*, a group of twenty-one people in San Jose, California, were treated for burns after walking barefoot over hot coals as part of an event called Unleash the Power Within, starring the motivational speaker Tony Robbins. "If you are anything like me," the article's author, Oliver Burkeman, wrote, "a cynical retort might suggest itself: What, exactly, did they expect would happen?"[9]

EPILOGUE

In today's era of nuclear and bacteriological weapons, regular armies are becoming less and less relevant. KGB General Aleksander Sakharovsky, who spent an unprecedented fourteen years as the Soviet Union's spy chief, used to preach that because "nuclear technology has made military force obsolete, terrorism should become our main weapon." The United States never will be a terrorist country. Therefore, our leaders in the White House, the Pentagon, and Congress are now debating how the United States can most effectively defeat the current nuclear threats to our country. That is all well and good, but few politicians seem to be paying enough attention to the power of intelligence, now a neglected weapon that at one time proved decisive in helping us win the Cold War without firing a shot.

In 1962, the Cuban Missile Crisis brought the U.S. to the brink of nuclear war. Today's history books correctly give credit to President Kennedy for averting that disaster. Readers thrill to tales of the U-2 spy planes that secretly overflew Cuba collecting vital information to counter Khrushchev's ambition to control the U.S. through nuclear missiles aimed at it. Lost in the euphoria over our victory, however, is the crucial role of the initial intelligence source, a courageous Soviet military intelligence officer named Oleg Penkovsky (the author of *The Penkovsky Papers*, (Collins, 1965). It was he who gave our intelligence community the tip that the Soviets were secretly installing nuclear weapons in Cuba, and it was his intelligence that enabled the United States to decode the images of the Soviet rockets that Khrushchev wanted to install secretly in Cuba, which our U-2 planes were then able to record. Unfortunately, Penkovsky was caught and executed by the KGB. His sacrifice, however, helped us avoid a nuclear war.

After the transformation of Russia into the first intelligence dictatorship in history and the birth of Islamic terrorism, our intelligence community did its best to persuade other enemy spy chiefs to join our intelligence community. A small ripple of intelligence defections followed, but in the 1980s the U.S. Congress prohibited the CIA from helping defectors—most of them resettled under protective identity—to publish in the United States. The result? To the best of our knowledge, no other enemy spy chief has followed in General Pacepa's path in the last forty years.

In our view, this prohibition —unique in the Western world—has been devastating for the United States. Some three thousand Americans were killed on September 11, 2001, because we did not have a defector, or a source in place that hoped to end his life as American citizen, at the top of al-Qaeda to tell us what its terrorist leaders were plotting. Over four thousand Americans died in Iraq because we did not have a top Iraqi source to tell us that Saddam Hussein did not have nuclear weapons.

Another two thousand American soldiers have so far died in Afghanistan, where the CIA's officers had to go disguised as civilian tourists on horseback in order to familiarize themselves with that virtually unknown terrorist country.[1] Russia's overnight occupation of Crimea also took our White House by surprise.

After 9/11, new public investigations raked our intelligence community over the coals. They did not focus on why we had no intelligence sources at the top of the Islamic terrorist organizations or on measures to correct that anomaly. Nor did they focus on how to increase the *trust* in our foreign intelligence community, although trust is the most valuable asset of any foreign intelligence service, no matter its nationality or political flavor. The 9/11 Commission devoted hundreds of pages to publicly blaming our intelligence community for not having identified the nineteen terrorists before they hijacked the airplanes, although terrorists entering the U.S. may be as elusive as needles in a haystack. Some 80 million passengers flew to the U.S. that year alone, on 823,757 commercial and 139,650 private flights; 330 million people crossed the Canadian and Mexican borders during that same year by car, train, and truck; and another 18 million entered the country by sea.[2]

Evidently, none of the members of Congress who authored the 585 pages of *The 9/11 Commission Report*, formally named *Final Report of the National Commission on Terrorist Attacks Upon the United States*, was familiar with the crucial role played by agents and defectors in foreign intelligence operations.

We hope that the president of the United States will correct that. We also hope he will take the CIA out of the daily news. A belled cat doesn't catch any mice.

BIOGRAPHICAL NOTES

AMBASSADOR R. JAMES WOOLSEY

R. James Woolsey Jr. is a lawyer and diplomat who was director of Central Intelligence from 1993 to 1995 under President Clinton.

He received his undergraduate degree from Stanford (Phi Beta Kappa), his master's degree from Oxford (where he was a Rhodes Scholar), and his law degree from Yale, where he was founder and president of Yale Citizens for Eugene McCarthy for President and prominently active in the anti–Vietnam War movement.

He was a captain in the U.S. Army and a program analyst in the Office of the Secretary of Defense, then held a variety of government positions in the 1970s and 1980s, including National Security Council staff and adviser with the U.S. Delegation to the Strategic Arms Limitation Talks and general counsel to the Committee on Armed Services for the U.S. Senate.

He was undersecretary of the Navy from 1977 to 1979 and was involved in treaty negotiations with the Soviet Union for five years in the 1980s. He was ambassador and U.S. representative for negotiations on conventional armed forces in Europe from 1989–91.

His career also has included time as a professional lawyer and venture capitalist.

LT. GENERAL ION MIHAI PACEPA

Lt. Gen. (ret.) Ion Mihai Pacepa is the highest-ranking intelligence official from an enemy country ever to have been granted political asylum in the United States. His defection made him the most hunted American citizen alive. Romania's tyrant, Nicolae Ceausescu, created a super-secret intelligence unit staffed with a thousand officers charged to kill Pacepa and set a $2 million bounty on his head. Libya's Muammar Qaddafi and the Palestine Liberation Organization's Yasser Arafat set other multi-million-dollar rewards.

In 1982, Ceausescu also hired the infamous terrorist Carlos the Jackal to kill Pacepa and to blow up with explosives the headquarters of Radio Free Europe in Munich, which was broadcasting Pacepa's revelations. At that time Carlos was famous for attacking the French embassy in the Hague, capturing the OPEC headquarters in Vienna, and firing rocket-propelled grenades the Orly Airport near Paris.

In mid-September 1980, the leaders of Hungarian foreign intelligence, which provided shelter in Budapest to Carlos, asked Moscow's approval for Pacepa's assassination. A few days later, Moscow informed them that the Soviet Politburo approved Pacepa's assassination.

On October 11, 1980, Carlos and his girlfriend, Magdalena Kopp, moved to Bucharest, where they lived in a villa owned by the Romanian political police, the Securitate. The next day the Romanian foreign intelligence service opened bank account # 47 11 210 350 2 at the Romanian Bank for Foreign Trade under the names "Michael Mallios" and "Anna Luise Toto-Kramer." They spent a month of training in Romania.

Carlos was unable to find Pacepa, but on February 21, 1981, he exploded a plastic bomb at RFE headquarters in Munich, injuring eight RFE employees. Five Romanian diplomats assigned to West Germany were expelled because of their involvement in this bloody operation. In a public speech, French president Francois Mitterrand called Romania's foreign intelligence service "a band of assassins" and postponed a scheduled official visit to Bucharest.

In 1994, Carlos was captured in Khartoum, Sudan, by the French counterintelligence service, the DST, with which Pacepa had cooperated after he defected. Carlos was sentenced to life in prison. He is currently incarcerated in Clairvaux Prison in France.

In May 2015, Pacepa's book *Disinformation*, coauthored with Professor Ronald Rychlak, was included among the best ten political books ever written, next to Solzhenitsyn's *The Gulag Archipelago* and Pasternak's *Doctor Zhivago*. In 2019, when Romania celebrated thirty years since the execution of Ceausescu, Pacepa's book *Red Horizons* was republished there as *The Golden Book of the War Against Communism*.

NOTES

INTRODUCTION

1 The Los Alamos National Laboratory, one of two U.S. facilities specializing in classified work on nuclear weapons design, recently published a never before seen pictorial report on those cities titled "History of Russian Nuclear Weapons Program" (http://fas.org/nuke /guide/russia/lanl-history.pdf)

2 "Putin: Soviet collapse a genuine tragedy," Associated Press, April 25, 2005, posted as http://www.nbcnews.com/id/7632057/ns/world_news/t /putin-soviet-collapse-genuine-tragedy/#.VXsOqLNlzzY.

3 (Translation: literally "appetite comes in eating," or to prod someone into eating when they don't feel like it.)

4 Doug Mainwaring, "We are all Tea Partiers now," *The Washington Times*, September 30, 2010, p.1.

5 "American capitalism gone with a whimper," *Pravda*, April 27, 2004.

CHAPTER ONE — SOCIALIST RUSSIA: AN "ILLEGAL" INTELLIGENCE TYRANNY

1 https://spectator.org/39264_hiding-behind-us-law/

2 *The History of Espionage*, chapter entitled "Günther Guillaume, Soviet Spy in West Germany," internet version, http://members.nbci.com/1spy.

3 In Soviet intelligence terminology, the term "illegal officer" designated an intelligence officer who was assigned under nonofficial cover, often—but not always—in alias.

4 http://revcom.us/socialistconstitution/

CHAPTER TWO — UNDERCOVER FEUDALISM IN THE TWENTIETH CENTURY

1 Mike Christopulos, "Russian Orthodox priest Father Arseny shone with Christ's light in Soviet prison camp," *The Sword*, vol. 1:36, August 2014.

2 Astolphe, marquis de Custine, *Journey For Our Time*, edited and translatedby Phyllis Penn Kohler. (Washington, DC: Regnery, 1987), 161, 152.

3 Quoted in Edward Hallet Carr, *The Bolshevik Revolution 1917–1923* (London: MacMillan, 1953), Vol. III, p. 14.

4   John Costello and Oleg Tsarev, *Deadly Illusions* (New York: Crown, 1993), p. 24.

5   This letter was seen by the author in 1992 at an exhibit entitled "Revelations from the Russian Archives," which was displayed at the Library of Congress, Washington, DC.

6   George Legget, *The Cheka: Lenin's Political Police*. (Oxford University Press, 1981), p. 114, as quoted in Andrew and Gordievsky, KGB, p. 44.

7   Quoted in Ronald W. Clark, *Lenin*. (New York: Harper & Row, 1988), pp. 472, 474.

8   On my visits to the Lubyanka, I was never taken to the KGB officers' club. The existence of the Dzerzhinsky memorial figure is confirmed in Andrew and Gordievsky, KGB, pp. 42–43, which adds that it was thrown out toward the end of Stalin's reign but that then under Khrushchev a huge statue of him was erected outside KGB headquarters on Dzerzhinsky Square.

9   Jean Mackenzie, "Anti-Semitism is resurfacing in Russia," *Boston Globe*, November 8, 1998, as published on the internet at www.fsumonitor.com /stories/11098mak.shtml

10 William Korey, "Russian Antisemitism, Pamyat, and the Demonology of Zionism," The Hebrew University of Jerusalem, as published on http:// sicsa.huji.ac.il/studies2.html.

11 The Okhrana was founded in 1881 by Alexander III. It replaced the Department of State Police, which failed to save the life of his father, Tsar Alexander II.

12 In 1894, French Captain Alfred Dreyfus, a wealthy Alsatian Jew, was falsely sentenced for espionage by an anti-Semitic court and deported to Devil's Island. Émile Zola, a leading supporter of Dreyfus, promptly published J'accuse, reproving the judges for their anti-Semitism. Zola was tried for libel but escaped to England. The violent partisanship over this case dominated French life for more than a decade.

13 Philip Grave, "The Protocols: A Literary Forgery," *The Times*, London, August 16, 17, and 18, 1921, as published in www.nizkor.org/ftp. cgi?documents/protocols/protocols.zion.

CHAPTER THREE — SOCIALIST ANTI-SEMITISM

1   Jean-Louis Panné, Andrzej Paczkowski, Karel Bartosek, Jean-Louis Margolin, Nicolas Werth, Stéphane Courtois, Mark Kramer (ed., tr.) and Jonathan Murphy (tr.), *The Black Book of Communism* (Harvard University Press, 1997).

2   "U.S. Department of State Annual Report on International Religious Freedom for 1999: Russia," September 9, 1999, internet edition.

3   Text of the U.S. Senate letter, including signatures listed alphabetically, published on the internet at http://www.us-israel.org/jsource /Histroy?Human%20Rights/98sens.html.

4   Steve Rosenberg, "Anti-Semitism alarms Russian Jews," BBC News, Moscow, as posted on http://news.bbc.co.uk/2/hi/europe/427183.stm.

5   Amiram Barkat and Gideon Alon, "Survey: Anti_Semitism rises in Russia, schrinks in Europe," *Haaretz*, January 27, 2006.

6   John Toland, *Adolf Hitler* (New York: Doubleday, 1976), p. 548.

7   Dekanozov can be seen next to Stalin in the official picture of the Soviet May Day parade published in *Pravda* on May 3, 1940.

8   Departamentul de Informatii Externe, Romania's espionage service.

CHAPTER FOUR — STEALING AMERICA'S NUCLEAR BOMB

1   This interpretation now appears in many places, most notably in John Earl Haynes, Harvey Klehr, and Alexander Vasiliev, Spies: The Rise and Fall of the KGB in America (New Haven: Yale University Press, 2009), 39–58.

2   Whittaker Chambers, *Witness* (Washington: Regnery, 1952, reissued), 271–280.

3   Chambers, *Witness*, 281–282.

4   Chambers, *Witness*, 445–446.

5   Allen Weinstein and Alexander Vassiliev, The Haunted Wood (New York: Modern Library, 2000), 183.

6   Haynes, Klehr, and Vassiliev, *Spies*, 46, 57.

7   Haynes, Klehr, and Vasiliev, *Spies*, 58.

8   Pavel Sudoplatov and Anatoli Sudoplatov, with Jerrold L. and Leona P. Schecter, *Special Tasks: The Memoirs of an Unwanted Witness—a Soviet Spymaster* (Boston: Little, Brown, 1994).

9   Unless noted otherwise, the information in this chapter regarding Oppenheimer's connection with Soviet foreign intelligence is taken from Pavel Sudoplatov's Special Tasks. Specific quotes are footnoted.

10 Herbert Romerstein and Eric Breindel, *The Venona Secrets: Exposing Soviet Espionage and America's Traitors* (Washington: Regnery, 2000), 257, 266, 277.

11 Sudoplatov, *Special Tasks*, 175–176.

12 Sudoplatov, *Special Tasks*, 194.

13 Sudoplatov, *Special Tasks*, 186–187.

14 Sudoplatov, *Special Tasks*, 184.

CHAPTER FIVE — DISINFORMATION: THE ORIGINAL FAKE NEWS

1   As in previous chapters on the Oppenheimer case, unless otherwise noted, all material in this chapter can be found in Pavel Sudoplatov's Special Tasks.

2   Sudoplatov, *Special Tasks*, 177.

3   Christopher Andrew and Vasili Mitrokhin, The Sword and the Shield: The Mitrokhin Archive and the Secret History of the KGB (New York: Basic Books, 1999).

4   John Earl Haynes, Harvey Klehr, and Alexander Vassiliev, *Spies: The Rise and Fall of the KGB in America* (New Haven: Yale University Press, 2009), 56–57. There are many references to Kheifetz and to the nonrecruitment of Oppenheimer in several books based on Vassiliev's documents.

5   Sudoplatov, *Special Tasks*, 197, 214, 218.

6   Andrew and Mitrokhin, The Mitrokhin Archive, 107–108, 122–124. The information on Zarubin's awards is attributed to Samolis (ed.), Veterany Vneshnei Razvedki Rosii [Veterans of Russian Foreign Intelligence], 53–55, not to Mitrokhin.

7   Haynes, Klehr, and Vassiliev, *Spies*, 529–530.

8   Sudoplatov, Special Tasks, 197.

9   Jerrold and Leona Schecter, *Sacred Secrets: How Soviet Intelligence Operations Changed American History* (Washington: Brassey's, 2002), 81–82.

10 Andrew and Mitrokhin, *The Mitrokhin Archive*, 123–124.

11 Sudoplatov, *Special Tasks*, 197.

12 Haynes, Klehr, and Vassiliev, *Spies*, 52.

13 Jerrold and Leona Schecter, *Sacred Secrets*, 315–317.

14 Sudoplatov, *Special Tasks*, 197.

15 The author has the original letter.

16 Herbert Romerstein and Eric Breindel, *The Venona Secrets: Exposing Soviet Espionage and America's Traitors*. (Washington: Regnery, 2000) 15–17

17 Christopher Andrew and Oleg Gordievsky, *KGB: The Inside Story of Its Foreign Operations from Lenin to Gorbachev*, (New York: HarperCollins, 1990), 287-288 and passim.

"DEVELOPING THE SECRET INK"

p. 3 The **"Walker Note"** – Commission Ex. 1: Unsigned note to Marina Oswald, in *Hearings Before the President's Commission on the Assassination of President Kennedy*, 88th Cong. 16:1 (1964), accessed September 14, 2020, www.govinfo.gov/features/warren-commission-report-and-hearings.

p. 5 **Photocopy of Oswald's Nov. 9, 1963, Letter** – Commission Ex. 15: Letter from Lee Harvey Oswald to the Russian Embassy, November 9, 1963, in *Hearings Before the President's Commission on the Assassination of President Kennedy*, 88th Cong. 16:33 (1964), accessed September 14, 2020, www.govinfo.gov/features/warren-commission-report-and-hearings.

p. 5 **Draft of the Same Letter Found in Ruth Paine's Garage** – Commission Ex. 103: Draft of letter written by Lee Harvey Oswald to the Russian Embassy, in *Hearings Before the President's Commission on the Assassination of President Kennedy*, 88th Cong. 16:443 (1964), accessed

September 14, 2020, www.govinfo.gov/features/warren-commission-report-and-hearings.

p. 6 **Esta Semana Cover & Photocopy** – Commission Ex. 2486: Photos of pamphlet entitled *This Week—Esta Semana*, for the week September 28–October 4, 1963, in *Hearings Before the President's Commission on the Assassination of President Kennedy*, 88th Cong. 25:683, 685 (1964), accessed September 14, 2020, www.govinfo.gov/features/warren-commission-report-and-hearings.

p. 6 **Oswald's Letter** – Commission Ex. 15: Letter from Lee Harvey Oswald to the Russian Embassy, November 9, 1963, in *Hearings Before the President's Commission on the Assassination of President Kennedy*, 88th Cong. 16:33 (1964), accessed September 14, 2020, www.govinfo.gov/features/warren-commission-report-and-hearings.

p. 7 **Letter Translation** – *Report of the President's Commission on the Assassination of President John F. Kennedy (Warren Commission Report)*, 88th Cong. 309-311 (1964), accessed September 14, 2020, www.govinfo.gov/features/warren-commission-report-and-hearings, U.S. Government Publishing Office, September 14, 2020.

p. 8 **Photocopy of Oswald's Address Book** – Commission Ex. 18: Address book of Lee Harvey Oswald, in *Hearings Before the President's Commission on the Assassination of President Kennedy*, 88th Cong. 16:53 (1964), accessed September 14, 2020, www.govinfo.gov/features/warren-commission-report-and-hearings.

p. 8 **U.S. Secret Service Report** – Commission Ex. 1143: Excerpt from Secret Service Report, August 28, 1964, in *Hearings Before the President's Commission on the Assassination of President Kennedy*, 88th Cong. 22:153 (1964), accessed September 14, 2020, www.govinfo.gov/features/warren-commission-report-and-hearings.

p. 9 **Photocopy of Russian Book** – Commission Ex. 1971: "Book of Useful Advice," in Russian, in *Hearings Before the President's Commission on the Assassination of President Kennedy*, 88th Cong. 23:828 (1964), accessed September 14, 2020, www.govinfo.gov/features/warren-commission-report-and-hearings.

p. 10 **Marina's Letter to the Russian Embassy** – Commission Ex. 12: Undated letter from Marina Oswald to the Russian Embassy, in *Hearings Before the President's Commission on the Assassination of President Kennedy*, 88th Cong. 16:25 (1964), accessed September 14, 2020, www.govinfo.gov/features/warren-commission-report-and-hearings.

p. 10 **Lee Harvey Oswald's Letter to the Russian Embassy** – Commission Ex. 13: Letter from Lee Harvey Oswald to the Russian Embassy, July 1, 1963, in *Hearings Before the President's Commission on the Assassination of President Kennedy*, 88th Cong. 16:30 (1964), accessed September 14, 2020, www.govinfo.gov/features/warren-commission-report-and-hearings.

p. 11 **Translation of Marina's Letter** – Commission Ex. 12: Undated letter from Marina Oswald to the Russian Embassy, in *Hearings Before the President's Commission on the Assassination of President Kennedy*, 88th Cong. 16:26, 28 (1964), accessed September 14, 2020, www.govinfo.gov/features/warren-commission-report-and-hearings.

p. 12 **Photocopies of Oswald's "Historic Diary"** – Commission Ex. 24: Lee Harvey Oswald's "Historic Diary," in *Hearings Before the President's Commission on the Assassination of President Kennedy*, 88th Cong. 16:94-95 (1964), accessed September 14, 2020, www.govinfo.gov/features/warren-commission-report-and-hearings.

p. 13 **Photocopies of Oswald's Letters** – Commission Ex. 252: Letter from Lee Harvey Oswald to the American Embassy in Moscow, May 1961, in *Hearings Before the President's Commission on the Assassination of President Kennedy*, 88th Cong. 16:705-06 (1964), accessed September 14, 2020, www.govinfo.gov/features/warren-commission-report-and-hearings.

p. 14 **Photocopies of Oswald's Letters to His Brother** – Commission Ex. 298: Letter from Lee Harvey Oswald to Robert Oswald, May 5, 1961, in *Hearings Before the President's Commission on the Assassination of President Kennedy*, 88th Cong. 16:826 (1964), accessed September 14, 2020, www.govinfo.gov/features/warren-commission-report-and-hearings.

p. 15 **Photocopy of Oswald's Photograph** – Commission Ex. 133-A: Photograph of Lee Harvey Oswald holding a rifle, May 5, 1961, in *Hearings Before the President's Commission on the Assassination of President Kennedy*, 88th Cong. 16:510 (1964), accessed September 14, 2020, www.govinfo.gov/features/warren-commission-report-and-hearings.

p. 15 **Back of Oswald's Photograph** – Ex. 133-A DEM: Reverse of photograph of Lee Harvey Oswald holding a rifle, in *Appendix to Hearings Before the Select Committee on Assassinations of the U.S. House of Representatives*, 95th Cong. 6:151 (1979), accessed September 14, 2020, https://history-matters.com/archive/contents/hsca/contents_hsca_vol6.htm.

p. 16 **De Mohrenschildt Manuscript** – Manuscript by George de Mohrenschildt, in *Appendix to Hearings Before the Select Committee on Assassinations of the U.S. House of Representatives*, 95th Cong. 12:255-56 (1979), accessed September 14, 2020, https://history-matters.com/archive/contents/hsca/contents_hsca_vol6.htm.

p. 17 **Title Page of Joesten/PGU Book** – Joachim Joesten, *Oswald: Assassin Or Fall Guy?* (New York: Marzani & Munsell, 1964), 2.

p. 18 **Joesten's Dedication Page** – Joachim Joesten, *Oswald: Assassin Or Fall Guy?* (New York: Marzani & Munsell, 1964), 3.

p. 19 **Dear Mr. Hunt Letter** – Ex. 47: Handwritten letter to Mr. Hunt, in *Appendix to Hearings Before the Select Committee on Assassinations of the U.S. House of Representatives*, 95th Cong. 8:357 (1979), accessed

September 14, 2020, https://history-matters.com/archive/contents/hsca/
contents_hsca_vol6.htm.

p. 20 **Photocopy of De Mohrenschildt's Manuscript** – Manuscript by George
de Mohrenschildt, in *Appendix to Hearings Before the Select Committee
on Assassinations of the U.S. House of Representatives*, 95th Cong. 12:204
(1979), accessed September 14, 2020, https://history-matters.com/
archive/contents/hsca/contents_hsca_vol6.htm.

CHAPTER SIX – THE KILLING OF PRESIDENT KENNEDY

1   https://en.wikipedia.org/wiki/Nikita_Khrushchev
2   Literaturnaya Gazeta, February 24, 1988, cited in Andrew and
     Gordievsky, p. 424.
3   Nikita Khrushchev, *Khrushchev Remembers*, translated and edited by
     Strobe Talbot (Boston: Little, Brown and Company, 1970), P. 337. (This
     is the first volume of Khrushchev's memoirs and will henceforth be
     referred to as Khrushchev I.)
4   Andrew and Gordievsky, p. 424.
5   Ion Mihai Pacepa, *Programmed to Kill*, (Chicago: Ivan R. Dee, 2007).
6   John Barron, *KGB: The Secret Work of Soviet Secret Agents* (New York:
     Reader's Digest Books, 1974, reprinted by Bamtam Books), p. 429.
7   The Kremlin's disinformation operation, codenamed Dragon, was
     described in my book *Programmed to Kill: Moscow's Responsibility for
     Lee Harvey Oswald's Assassination of President John Fitzgerald Kennedy*.
     In 2010, this book was presented at the Organization of American
     Historians conference with a review by Prof. Stan Weber (McNeese State
     University), describing it as "a superb new paradigmatic work on the
     death of President Kennedy" and a "must read for everyone interested
     in the assassination," from the "most casual reader to the serious student
     preparing his or her own magnum opus."
8   Stan Weber, "A New Paradigmatic Work on the JFK Assassination,"
     H-Net Online, October 2009, http://www.h-net.org/reviews/showrev.
     php?id=25348. In 2010, Pacepa's book *Programmed to Kill* was presented
     at the Organization of American Historians conference. Prof. Stan
     Weber (McNeese State University) described it as a "must read for
     everyone interested in the assassination."
9   WC Report, pp. 183–187.
10 WCE 1.
11 WC Vol. 1, p. 17.
12 WC Report, p. 183.
13 Warren Commission Exhibit 2486.
14 Testimony of Ruth Hyde Paine, Warren Commission Vol. 3, pp. 12–13.
15 Warren Commission Exhibit 1400.
16 Priscilla Johnson McMillan, *Marina and Lee* (New York: Harper & Row,
     1977), p. 496.

17   Edward Jay Epstein, *Legend: The Secret World of Lee Harvey* Oswald
     (New York: Reader's Digest Press), p. 16.
18   George J. Church, "Crawling with Bugs," *Time*, April 20, 1987, pp. 14–24.
19   Molly Moore and David B. Ottaway, "2nd Ranking Embassy Marine A
     Suspect in Security Breach," *The Washington Post*, April 1, 1987, pp. A1,
     A19.
20   Kritika Explorations in Russian and Eurasian History 14(2):279-312, as
     published in http://www.researchgate.net/publication/270617204
     _Khrushchev%27s_Second_First_Secretaries_Career_Trajectories_after
     _the_Unification_of_Oblast_Party_Organizations

CHAPTER SEVEN – GHEORGHIU-DEJ, CEAUSESCU, AND "RADU"

1   Vladimir Kuzichkin, *Inside the KGB: My Life in Soviet Espionage* (New
     York: Pantheon Books, 1990), pp. 215–218.
2   For details on General Militaru's recruitment by Soviet intelligence see
     Pacepa, Red Horizons, pp.193–5 and 201–2.
3   *Der Spiegel*, November 9, 1987, p. 186
4   Dumitru Mazilu, "Revolutia Furata ("The Stolen Revolution"), serialized
     in Lumea Libera (New York), July 27, 1991, p. 9
5   Vladimir Tismaneanu, *Reinventing Politics: Eastern Europe from Stalin to
     Havel* (New York: The Free Press, 1992), p. 234.
6   Andrei Codrescu, *The Hole in the Flag: A Romanian Exile's Story of
     Return and Revolution* (New York: William Morrow and Company, Inc.,
     1991), pp. 47–8.
7   "Ion Iliescu: Romania's ex-leader charged with crimes against humanity,"
     World Justice News, April 20, 2019.

CHAPTER EIGHT – THE GLASNOST SWINDLE

1   Zhores Medvedev, *Gorbachev* (New York: Norton, 1987), p. 37.
2   Vladimir Solovyov and Elena Klepikova, *Behind the High Kremlin's Wall.*
     (New York: Dodd, Mead, 1987), pp. 173–6.
3   Christian Schmidt-Häuer, *Gorbachev: The Path to Power* (London: I. B.
     Tauris, 1987), p. 64.
4   Tolkovyy SlovarRusskogo Yazyka (Explanatory Dictionary of the Russian
     Language), ed. D.N. Ushakov (Moscow: "Soviet Encyclopedia" State
     Institute, 1935), Vol. I, p. 570.
5   GLASNOST: Dostupnost obshchestvennomy obsuzhdeniyu, kontrolyu;
     publichnost (meaning, the quality of being made available for public
     discussion or control), Tolkovyy SlovarRusskogo Yazyka (Explanatory
     Dictionary of the Russian Language), ed. D.N. Ushakov (Moscow: "Soviet
     Encyclopedia" State Institute, 1935), Vol. I, p. 570.
6   Sam Marcy, "The collapse of the USSR and the destiny of socialism,"
     www.nytransfer@icg.apc.org, pp. 12–13.
7   Cal Thomas, "20/20 hindsight and insight," *The Washington Times*,
     March 24, 2002, internet edition.

8   David Wise, "Closing Down the KGB," *The New York Times Magazine*, November 24, 1991, pp. 68, 71.

9   Uri Dan and Leo Standora, "KGB claims it has no record on Rosenbergs," *The New York Post*, November 25, 1991, p. 1.

10 (State Security Organs), internet, fsb.ru/history/organi, p. 2.

11 (State Security Organs), internet, fsb.ru/history/organi, p. 2.

12 Natalia Gevorkian, "Revanchism in the Security Forces," Crossroads: A Monitor of Post-Soviet Reform, March 15, 1993, p.4.

13 "Russian successor to KGB gains extensive powers, alarming right activists," *The Baltimore Sun*, April 7, 1995, p. 6A.

14 John Lloyd, "The Russian Devolution," *The New York Times Magazine*, August 15, 1999, p. 38.

15 Richard Lourie, "Who Stole Russia?" *The Washington Post Book World*, October 15, 2000, p. 3.

16 "Could it lead to fascisms?" *The Economist*, July 11, 1998, U.S. edition, p. 19.

17 Yevgenia Albats, *The KGB: The State Within a State* (New York: Farrar, Straus, Giroux, 1994), pp.23.

18 Yevgenia Albats, "Democratic Façade in Russia," *The Washington Post*, June 6, 2000, p. B7.

19 "The Perils of Catching Cold," *Time*, December 1997, p. 38, Internet Edition, geocities.com/CapitolHill/Lobby/9802/yelt1.

20 "Can the crisis end in a coup?" Moscow, the Nezavisimaya Gazyeta, July 7, 1998, p. 1.

21 Barry Renfrew, "Boris Yeltsin Resigns," *The Washington Post*, December 31, 1999, 6:48 a.m.

22 The Drudge Report, December 31, 1999, 11:00 a.m. UTC.

23 Robert Amsterdam, Obama and McCain Fumble Russian Debate, October 9, 2008 http://www.robertamsterdam.com/2008/10/obama _and_mccain_both_fumble_r.htm.

24 "Russians tune up for Soviet-style start of the New Year," AFP, Moscow, December 31, 2000, internet edition.

CHAPTER NINE — AS RUSSIAN AS THE BALALAIKA

1   "Clan of FSB Provide a 'Foundation' for the Putin Regime," Novaya Gazeta, June 2003, republished by Center for the Future of Russia.

2   "The Return of the KGB," Center for the Future of Russia, March 23, 2003, p. 1.

3   Michael R. Gordon, "Putin, in a Rare Interview, Says He'll Use Ex-K.G.B. Aides to Root Out Graft," *The New York Times*, March 24, 2000, internet edition, p. 2.

4   http://online.wsj.com/news/articles/SB121824156547126077

5   Douglas J. Brown, "Chekists Around the World Celebrate 9/11," NewsMax.com, September 19, 2002, published in www.newsmax.com /archives/articles/2002/18/170000.shtml.

6   http://spectator.org/archives/2009/06/26/an-open-letter-to-the-psdrn
    -ge
7   http://www.cnbc.com/id/101852656
8   http://online.wsj.com/news/articles/SB121824156547126077
9   http://www.washingtonpost.com/world/putin-changes-course-admits
    -russian-troops-were-in-crimea-before-vote/2014/04/17/b3300a54-c617
    -11e3-bf7a-beo1a9b69cf1_story.html
10 http://www.cnbc.com/id/101852656
11 Julius Strauss, "False teeth for children of Stalin's victims," *The Age*,
    January 29, 2003, published on the internet at www.theage.comau
    /articles/2003/01/28/1043534055349.html.
12 "What happened to Kursk," www.aeronautics.ru., synopsis.
13 "Russian Elite's Old Reflexes," *Izvestiya*, August 18, 2000, p. 1.
14 "Kursk Submarine Disaster: Russian Elite Scored, Democracy Tested,"
    www.usinfo.state.gov-admin/005.
15 "Sub's Crew Are Victims Of Putin's Misplaced Pride," *Daily Express*, lead
    editorial, August 18, 2000.
16 *Journey for Our Time: The Russian Journals of the Marquis de Custine*,
    edited and translated by Phyllis Penn Kohler. (Washington, D.C.: 1987),
    Gateway Editions, p. 171.
17 "Chernobyl—the accident," internet, www.bellona.no/12663.
18 Graham Young, "Chernobyl: The Disaster and its Legacy," internet,
    www.geocities.com/graham-young-uk/Chernobyl.html., chapter on
    environmental and health implications.
19 Joe Topino, "Putin could be world's richest man with stolen 200 Billion
    fortune," *New York Post*, February 16, 2015.
20 "Putin offers sympathy and support for US," Radio Free Europe Newsline,
    September 12, 2001, internet edition.
21 Oleg Kalugin, *The First Directorate: My 32 Years in Intelligence and
    Espionage Against the West* (New York: St. Martins Press, 1994).
22 Leonid Berres, "Oleg Kalugin to Be Tried in Absentia," trans. Vitaly
    Baskakov, Kommersant, June 5, 2002, p.1
23 http://spectator.org/archives/2009/06/26/an-open-letter-to-the-psdrn
    -ge
24 "Defector: Putin's KGB trained Top al-Qaeda Terrorist," written by staff,
    The New American, August 8, 2006, http://www.thenewamerican.com
    /world-news/europe/item/15162-defector-putin-s-kgb-trained-top-al
    -qaeda-terrorists.
25 John Lloyd, "The Logic of Vladimir Putin," *The New York times* Magazine,
    March 19, 2000, P. 65.
26 Celestine Bohlen, "Putin Tells Why He Became a Spy," *The New York
    Times*, March 11, 2000, internet edition, p. 2.
27 Miriam Elder, "The Only Show in Town," *The New York Times*, Book
    Review, Special Issue, November 30, 2014, p. 14.

28 "PARTIAL JUSTICE: An inquiry into the deaths of journalists in Russia, 1993–2009, IFJ Bruxelles, June 2009.

CHAPTER TEN – THE "DRAGON" OPERATION

1 Lt. Gen. Ion Mihai Pacepa, *Programmed to Kill: Lee Harvey Oswald, the Soviet Kgb, and the Kennedy Assassination,* (Chicago: Ivan R Dee, 2007).

2 Exhibits of documents of the Warren Commission investigation, Vol 13, p. 986.

3 Epstein, *Legend,* p. 25.

4 Epstein, *Legend,* p. 25.

5 HSCA Report, pp. 100-103.

6 Boris Yeltsin, *The Struggle for Russia,* translated from the Russian by Catherine A. Fitzpatrick (New York: Times Books, a division of Random House, 1994), 305–309.

7 Ion Mihai Pacepa, *Programmed to Kill* Lee Harvey Oswald, the Soviet KGB, and the Kennedy Assassination (Chicago: Ivan R. Dee, 2007).

8 Christopher Andrew and Vasili Mitrokhin, *The Sword and the Shield: The Mitrokhin Archive and the Secret History of the KGB* (New York: Basic Books, 1999), 287–293. This archive contains reproductions of genuine documents found in the archives of the KGB's foreign intelligence directorate that were copied and then smuggled out to the West in 1993 by KGB archivist Vasili Mitrokhin.

9 John Barron, *Operation Solo: The FBI's Man in the Kremlin* (Washington, D.C.: Regnery, 1996), 104.

10 Max Holland, "How Moscow Undermined the Warren Commission," *The Washington Post,* November 22, 2003.

11 Andrew and Mitrokhin, *The Mitrokhin Archive,* 226–227.

12 Andrew and Mitrokhin, *The Mitrokhin Archive,* 228–229.

13 József Cardinal Mindszenty, *Memoirs,* translated by Richard and Clara Winston (New York: Macmillan, 1974), 114–117.

14 Barron, *Operation Solo: The FBI's Man in the Kremlin,* 91.

15 Edward Jay Epstein, *Legend: The Secret World of Lee Harvey Oswald* (New York: Reader's Digest Press, McGraw-Hill, 1978), 235, 324–325.

16 Brian Latell, *Castro's Secrets: Cuban Intelligence, the CIA, and the Assassination of John F. Kennedy* (New York: Palgrave Macmillan, 2012), 103, 215–216.

17 Latell, *Castro's Secrets,* 204–212, 218, 230.

18 All the information on this incident is taken from Barron, *Operation Solo: The FBI's Man in the Kremlin,* 97–104.

19 Vincent Bugliosi, *Reclaiming History: The Assassination of President John F. Kennedy* (New York: W. W. Norton, 2007), 324; Barron, *Operation Solo: The FBI's Man in the Kremlin,* 102.

20 John Barron, *Operation Solo: The FBI's Man in the Kremlin* (Washington, D.C.: Regnery, 1996). Unless stated otherwise, all information about the Childs brothers is taken from this book.

21 Mitrokhin Archive, 287–293 discusses the Childs brothers, but the material must be read carefully, because Mitrokhin's coauthor Christopher Andrew fills in the story from various other sources, especially Barron's *Operation Solo: The FBI's Man in the Kremlin*, that are identified only in the copious endnotes.

22 All the information in this chapter about Jack Childs and his various trips and meetings with Fidel Castro is taken from John Barron's *Operation Solo: The FBI's Man in the Kremlin*, 90–117.

CHAPTER ELEVEN – THE DESIGNATED HIT MAN

1 Except where specifically noted otherwise, the information given here on Oswald can be found fully sourced in Pacepa's *Programmed to Kill*.

2 "How Powers's plane was shot down," http://www.webslivki.com/ull.html (Russian). Morton Kelly, "Gary Powers and the U-2 incident," About. com.guide, *American History*, published as http://americanhistory.about. com/od/coldwar/a/gary_powers.htm.

3 "Anton's" case is related by John Barron in *KGB: The Secret World of Soviet Secret Agents* (New York: Reader's Digest Press, 1974), 321–330. "Anton's" true name is not given in order to protect him in his new life after his arrest by the Canadians.

4 All the factual material in this chapter can be found fully sourced in Pacepa's *Programmed to Kill*.

5 HSCA Vol. 12, p. 204.

6 Glenn Frankel, "Anti-Americanism Moves to West Europe's Political Mainstream," *The Washington Post*, February 10, 2003, as published on the internet by The World Revolution (www.worldrevolution.org /projects/webguide.asp?ID=555).

7 Departamentul de Informatii Externe, Romania's foreign intelligence service.

8 Herbert Romerstein, Soviet Active Measures and Propaganda, Mackenzie Institute Paper no. 17 (Toronto, 1989), pp. 14–15, 25–26. WPC Peace Courier, 1989, no. 4, as cited in Andrew and Gordievsky, KGB, p. 629.

9 Christopher Andrew and Oleg Gordievsky, *KGB: The Inside Story* (New York: Harper Collins, 1990), pp.432–433.

10 Documents of the Ninth Congress of the Communist Party of India, 1971 (New Delhi: Communist Party Publications, 1972), p. 414.

CHAPTER TWELVE – FROM PRESIDENTIAL ASSASSINATION TO INTERNATIONAL TERRORISM

1 Christopher Andrew and Oleg Gordievsky, *KGB: The Inside Story* (New York: Harper Collins, 1990), p. 545.

2 Craig R. Whitney, "East's Archives Reveal Ties to Terrorists," *The New York Times*, July 15, 1990, p. 6.

3   Raymond Ibrahim, "The Rape of Christopher Stevens," September 16, 2012, https://www.frontpagemag.com/fpm/144305/rape-christopher -stevens-raymond-ibrahim.

4   Stephen Schwartz, "John Christopher Stevens, 1960–2012: A Northern California Hero," *Huffington Post*, October 10, 2012.

CHAPTER THIRTEEN – THE KING IS DEAD! LONG LIVE THE KING!

1   The "convention" mentioned by Voroshilov was the 1925 Geneva Protocol prohibiting bacteriological weapons.

2   Walter Duranty, "Soviet threatens to use gas in was," *The New York Times*, February 23, 1938.

3   Geneva Biological Weapons Convention (BWC), updated in December 2017, prohibits the research and production of bacteriological weapons.

4   Vladimir Putin, "Being Strong: National Security Guarantees for Russia," as posted on February 20, 1992, at http://rt.com/politics/officil-world /strong-putin-military-russia-711.

5   List of Soviet BW institutions, programs and projects, Wikipedia,

6   "Video of the week: We have to pass the bill so you can find out what is in it," The Heritage Foundation, March 10, 2010, posted as: http://blog. heritage.org/2010/03/10/video-of-the-week-we-have-to-pass-the-bill-so -you-can-find-what-is-in-it/

7   Deroy Murdock, "Obama Occupies Wall Street," *National Review Online*, December 5, 2011.

8   David Satter, "100 Years of Communism—and 100 Million Dead," Hudson Institute,November 6, 2017.

9   Oliver Burkeman, "The Power of Negative Thinking," *The New York Times Sunday Review*, August 4, 2012, http://www.nytimes.com/2012/08/05/ opinion/sunday/the-positive-power-of-negative-thinking.html.

EPILOGUE

1   https://www.washingtonpost.com/news/worldviews/ wp/2015/06/03/149000-people-have-died-in-war-in-afghanistan-and -pakistan-since-2001-report-says/?utm_term=.5cee7861c1d8

2   Arnold de Borchgrave, "Sea no evil," *The Washington Times*, March 15, 2005, Commentary.

BIOGRAPHICAL NOTES

1   Cummings, p. 119.

2   Cummings, pp. 104-106.

3   "Plesita, o bruta securista" (Plesita, a Securitate beast), Ziua, Bucharest, February 19, 2000, internet edition.

4   Matei Pavel Haiducu, J'ai refuse de tuer: Un agent secret roumain revele les dessous de l'affaire, (I refused to kill: A Romanian secret agent reveals what was behind "the affair") (Paris: Librairie Plon, 1984).

5   Direction de la Surveillance du Territoire (Directorate of Territorial Surveillance). On July 1, 2008, it was merged into the current Direction Centrale du Renseignement Intérieur.

INDEX